This book is for all the mothers, fathers and caregivers who make careful, loving meal preparation part of their busy lives...

...and for the thousands of Pampered Chef Kitchen Consultants who help make the lives of everyday cooks a little easier and a lot more fun.

Doris Christopher
Founder and President of The Pampered Chef

BUSY MOM'S

COOKBOOK

with Doris Christopher

ACKNOWLEDGMENTS

With special thanks to:

Our friends at Time-Life Custom Publishing

Our test kitchen staff, who helped me create
the wonderful, timesaving recipes in this book

My husband, Jay, and daughters, Julie and Kelley, for their support
during my "busy mom" years

First printing. Printed in U.S.A.

For more information about Pampered Chef products, contact your
local Pampered Chef Consultant or a Pampered Chef
Customer Service representative at (630) 261-8850

The Pampered Chef, Ltd.
350 S. Rohlwing Road
Addison, IL 60101

The Pampered Chef® is a registered trademark
of The Pampered Chef, Ltd.

Time-Life is a trademark of Time Warner Inc. U.S.A.

The Deluxe Turkey Club Pizza recipe
on page 71 is reprinted with permission
of The Pillsbury Company, 1996.

The Chicken Quesadillas recipe
on page 83 is reprinted with permission
of the Campbell® Soup Company, 1996.

THE PAMPERED CHEF

BUSY MOM'S
COOKBOOK

with Doris Christopher

Busy Mom's Cookbook was produced
by Time-Life Custom Publishing exclusively for The Pampered Chef

CONTENTS

*Three-Step Pizza
(see page 18)*

Dinners

*South of the Border Supper
(see page 20)*

Breakfasts, Lunches and Snacks

Breakfast with a Twist (see page 64)

Soup and Sandwich Combo (see page 73)

INTRODUCTION

Is there such a thing these days as a mom—or a dad, for that matter—who **isn't** busy? From the moment we get up in the morning, it seems, we're on the run: to work, to school, to lessons and practices and games, to church and neighborhood activities. And that doesn't even begin to count housecleaning, laundry, yardwork, grocery shopping—and cooking.

Yes, life is almost certainly more hectic today than it was for our parents, and that means it's getting harder and harder to find time to sit down for one of the best family traditions of all: a good, old-fashioned family meal, a chance to gather together and share lively conversation and fresh, home-cooked food. But now, more than ever with today's busy lifestyles, families **need** that break—even if it's only for a few minutes. We need to stop and connect with one another, to replenish our energy, to remember how important we are to each other.

Yet who has time to cook anymore? Under all the pressures, even the most avid home chef can find meal preparation little more than a responsibility, a chore; I know I did. And with the variety of fast-food restaurants and takeout meals available these days, it's tempting to just stop and grab dinner on the way home. In a pinch, that's a great alternative. As a way of life, though, it's

> **"Home cooking is an old-fashioned idea that never really went out of style—and for good reason."**

expensive—and it's not exactly nutritious.

Cooking Can Be Fun Again

That's where I hope this book will come in. It's filled with an exciting variety of menus for breakfast, lunch, snacktime and dinner, all designed to be on your table 30 minutes after you start preparing them. These are meals that are different enough to entice your family, but not so exotic that your husband and kids will peer suspiciously at the food before daring to taste it. Even the most finicky will be asking for more! Developed and tested right here in our Pampered Chef kitchen, the recipes are easy to follow and feature healthy, everyday ingredients you can find in any grocery store.

In fact, to make things even easier for you, we've organized

"It's so important for families to find time to connect around the dinner table again."

those ingredients into two types of lists. The first, which you'll find here in the Introduction, is my "pantry list," or those products that I always have on hand in my kitchen. The second, which appears in a box with each menu throughout the book, is a smaller "shopping list" of only the extra things you might need to prepare that particular meal. In other words, if an ingredient appears on the Pantry List, it would not be repeated on the Shopping List.

These recipes are so easy, you almost don't need directions—but of course we provide them for you anyway, accompanied

Doris's Pantry List

Over the years, I've found that if I keep my refrigerator and cupboard stocked with the ingredients on this list, I generally have most of what I need to make an unlimited variety of meals. When I run out of one of these items, it goes right on my shopping list for the next week!

Spices and Seasonings

Almond Extract
Basil, dried
Bay Leaves
Chili Powder
Cinnamon, ground
Dill Weed
Italian Seasoning
Mustard, dry
Nutmeg, ground
Oregano, dried
Paprika
Pepper, black and hot red flakes
Rosemary, dried
Sage, dried
Salt
Thyme
Vanilla Extract

Condiments

Honey
Hot Pepper Sauce
Ketchup
Maple Syrup
Mayonnaise
Mild Salsa
Mustard, yellow and Dijon
Oil, vegetable and olive
Parmesan Cheese
Peanut Butter
Raisins
Soy Sauce
Vinegar, cider and red wine
Worcestershire Sauce

Basics

Baking Powder
Baking Soda
Beef Broth
Bread Crumbs
Canned Beans (kidney, baked, black, pinto)
Chicken Broth
Cornmeal
Cornstarch
Flour, all-purpose and whole wheat
Garlic
Lemons
Nonstick Vegetable Spray
Sugar, white, brown and powdered
Tomato Paste
Tomato Sauce
Tomatoes, whole canned

by clear, how-to photographs and some suggestions on how to combine steps to make the meal most efficiently. We also suggest some Pampered Chef products that can make your preparation even simpler. You'll find an illustrated glossary of some of our

"Our versatile Kitchen Cutters were great for clipping delicious sounding recipes, but then I could never find the recipes when I needed them. The Busy Mom's Cookbook is a collection of recipes that's handy, organized —and reliably good."

most versatile tools at the back of this book. Finally, you'll find helpful tips, including some handy money- and time-saving ideas, from me scattered throughout the book. Actually, this is the cookbook I could have used 12 or 13 years ago, when **my** life was at its busiest. Back then, I was putting a lot of energy into expanding the Pampered Chef business, but my two daughters were still in grammar school, so I wanted to be available for them, as well. I'd typically spend the day in my office (which was still in our home) doing paperwork, picking out new products, or talking with our Kitchen Consultants, and then I'd stop in the

afternoon when the girls got back from school. That was **our** time—the time when they'd change their clothes, have a snack, and join me in the kitchen to talk about their day and help me as I got dinner started.

Getting the Family to Help

We didn't always eat as a family of four in those days, since many nights I was out presenting Kitchen Shows. Often I'd fix something for my husband Jay and the girls to share, or I'd eat with them before I went out and he'd catch something later. There were times when Jay and I were like ships in the night! But we'd try to have a true family dinner at least once a week, and always on the weekends. As for the girls and me, those afternoons in the kitchen did give us the chance to share some time in a relaxed way as we put the evening meal together.

This has always been a tradition for us; I got Julie and Kelley involved in the kitchen from a very early age. I think every busy parent has to. No woman, or man, can be the family superhero, trying to do everything for everyone. It's physically impossible, and it's also just not fair!

10

Engaging children in some of the simpler tasks around the house gives them a sense of accomplishment and pride in their abilities, as well as an idea of what it takes to keep a household running smoothly, and why each family member should have a part in it.

At first, kids can do the most basic things—set the table, for instance, or bring you items from the pantry or refrigerator. As they get older, you can put them to work mixing batter or eggs or layering ingredients in a casserole. I was always amazed at how intently my girls watched the whole cooking process, just waiting for the moment when their step would come in. Having even a small task

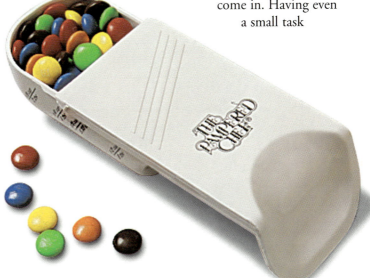

"Your family will be surprised and delighted with the interesting new ways you prepare even the simplest of foods, like snacks for birthday parties, Brownie meetings or after-school get-togethers."

in a recipe really involved them in the preparation of the entire meal and made them more interested in the outcome. It was almost like a science experiment!

Spending time with your kids in the kitchen may also give you the opportunity to introduce numbers (to very young children) and the concept of proportions (to the older ones), by having them measure out flour or salt or milk. Our all-in-one Adjustable Measuring Spoons and Wondercups make it simple for kids to figure out the right amount (and put an end to rummaging in the drawer for the proper size).

Many of our other tools are child-friendly, as well:

• The Kid's Pumpkin Cutter is designed especially for kids to use when carving pumpkins, but it works equally well on vegetables or fruit.

• The Apple Peeler/Corer/Slicer is a marvelous device for children (once Mom or Dad gets it set up and puts the apple in place). They **love** turning the handle and watching the peel curl off the fruit—and they're rewarded for their "work" with a nutritious snack.

• The Cut-N-Seal is another fun tool, and it produces magical results. Somehow peanut butter and jelly seems so much more exotic when it's made into moon-shaped pieces of bread!

"Children will love seeing—and eating!— the magical results they get from tools like the Apple Peeler/Corer/ Slicer and the Cut-N-Seal."

Mapping Out a Menu

But getting help with meal preparation is only half the battle. If you're like me, you still need to figure out **what** to make each day for dinner (and for a special breakfast or lunch, for that matter). Perhaps, like me, you get ideas from all sorts of places—you clip recipes from magazines and newspapers; you thumb through different cookbooks; and you ask friends to share their favorites, since everyone knows that's where the best recipes come from. The only problem with this practice is that you end up with a million different clippings and recipes everywhere!

And maybe, like me, you try to do some menu planning to help make life feel more organized day-to-day, and to help you stay

within your family's grocery budget. Years ago, when my daughters were still living at home, I had a pretty standard routine: Every week, I'd sit down with the Food section of our newspaper, clipping coupons and making a note of what was on sale or in season. Then I'd plan a week of menus, figuring out which ingredients I could use more than once (if I needed chopped onions for spaghetti sauce on Monday, for instance, I'd chop the whole onion and save or freeze what was left for another meal.

of zucchini right into it, stir in your other ingredients, and pour the batter for a zucchini bread right into the pan—without ever using another bowl. Believe me, no one hates cleanup more than me!

Bringing Your Family Back to the Table

My hope is that by providing a wealth of ideas for quick, easy, delicious meals, this cookbook will help you find more time—time with your children, time with your spouse, even time by yourself. I'd love for you to think of it as a textbook, of sorts, for busy parents—a single volume that will feel like a collection of recipes and tips from a good friend, the one place you know you can always turn to for a reliable recipe that will be simple to make and a pleasure to serve. My dream is that it will help make cooking fun again, even for the cooks who are most pressed for time, and, perhaps more important, it will help bring families back to the table again—a wonderful tradition that should be preserved for generations to come.

This strategy was not only economical, but it also produced delicious meals, because we all know that fresh food, at the height of its season, is what tastes best, no matter how you prepare it. It also helped me to vary the routine a little, so I wasn't serving the same six or seven dishes over and over. And, it saved precious time: By carefully thinking through all the ingredients I would need for a given week's meals, I was able to minimize extra midweek runs to the market to pick up one or two special things for a certain dish.

"It is possible to serve delicious, well-balanced meals, even if you don't have a lot of time. All it takes is a little organization and some cooperation from your family."

And isn't that what all busy parents need most, more time? Even our products can help in this regard, since many are designed to eliminate steps in the food preparation process. Take the Classic 2-Qt. Batter Bowl, with its easy-to-read measurements on the side. You can grate the appropriate amount

Doris Christopher
Doris Christopher
Founder and President of
The Pampered Chef

DINNERS

I think you'll be delighted to add these dinner recipes to your collection of family favorites. They're easy, tasty and nutritious, and—perhaps most important—they're versatile: You can make them ahead, freeze them for later, dress up the leftovers with a fresh salad or pack them into school lunches. What more could a busy parent want?

Chicken Skillet Dinner

TOMATO CHICKEN ITALIANO • EGG NOODLES WITH BUTTER
BERRY CRUMBLE • MILK

You'll need only two pots for this meal: one for the noodles and one for the chicken, which is simmered in a zucchini–red pepper tomato sauce. And for dessert, you can mix both the fruit and the oatmeal topping in the same Classic 2-Qt. Batter Bowl!

Grocery List

1 lb. boneless chicken breast halves
1 medium zucchini
1 medium red bell pepper
1 can (14½ oz.) diced tomatoes with Italian-style herbs

2 cups blueberries
2 cups raspberries
Quick oats
Butter
Vanilla ice cream

Pantry Items

All-purpose flour
Salt
Ground black pepper
Olive oil
Garlic

Dried basil
Sugar
Lemon juice
Brown sugar

16

Tomato Chicken Italiano

3 tablespoons all-purpose flour

½ teaspoon salt

¼ teaspoon ground black pepper

1 pound boneless chicken
breast halves

2 tablespoons olive oil

2 garlic cloves, pressed

1 cup cubed zucchini (about
1 medium zucchini)

1 cup red bell pepper chunks
(about 1 medium bell pepper)

2 teaspoons dried basil

1 can (14½ ounces) diced tomatoes
with Italian-style herbs

In 1-Quart Batter Bowl, combine flour, salt and black pepper. Dredge chicken in flour mixture, shaking off excess. Heat 1 tablespoon of the oil in 10-inch Generation II Frying Pan over medium heat. Add chicken and cook, turning once, until golden brown, about 10 minutes. Transfer chicken to a plate.

Add remaining 1 tablespoon oil and garlic to pan and cook, stirring constantly, until fragrant, about 30 seconds. Add zucchini, bell pepper and basil. Continue to cook, stirring, until vegetables are crisp-tender, about 2 minutes. Add tomatoes and stir. Return chicken to pan and cook until chicken is no longer pink in center and vegetables are tender, about 6 more minutes. Serve hot.

Yield: 4 servings

Berry Crumble

½ cup granulated sugar

2 tablespoons all-purpose flour

2 cups fresh blueberries

2 cups fresh raspberries

2 tablespoons lemon juice

1 cup quick or old-fashioned
oats, uncooked

¼ cup firmly packed brown sugar

½ cup butter or margarine,
cut into small pieces

Vanilla ice cream

Preheat oven to 350°F. Combine granulated sugar and flour in Classic 2-Qt. Batter Bowl. Using Mix 'N Scraper, gently fold in blueberries, raspberries and lemon juice. Spoon into Deep Dish Baker.

Combine oats and brown sugar in same Batter Bowl. Using Pastry Blender, cut butter into oat mixture until butter pieces are size of small peas. Sprinkle topping over berries. Bake 40 to 45 minutes or until filling is bubbling around edges and topping is nicely browned. Serve warm in bowls with scoops of vanilla ice cream on top.

Yield: 4 to 6 servings

Three-Step Pizza

THREE-STEP PIZZA • GARDEN SALAD
DEVILISH BROWNIE SUNDAES • SOFT DRINKS

Why call out for pizza when you can have a fresh, hot one in the same amount of time? While it's baking, combine the brownie mix and some irresistible extras, like white and dark chocolate chips, for an unbelievably good dessert.

Grocery List

1 package (10 oz.) refrigerated pizza crust dough
Pizza sauce
2 cups shredded mozzarella cheese
1 cup fresh vegetables
¼ cup cooked meat

1 box (21 to 24 oz.) brownie mix
Chocolate chips
Butterscotch sauce
White chocolate chips
Vanilla ice cream
Chocolate sauce

Pantry Items

Cornmeal
Grated Parmesan cheese

Nonstick vegetable spray

18

1 tablespoon cornmeal

1 package (10 ounces) refrigerated pizza crust dough

¾ cup pizza sauce

2 cups shredded mozzarella cheese

¼ cup grated Parmesan cheese

1 cup chopped fresh vegetables

¼ cup cooked meat

Three-Step Pizza

Preheat oven to 400°F.

Step 1: Sprinkle cornmeal onto 13-inch Round Baking Stone. Unroll dough and place on cornmeal. Starting in center, roll dough into a 12-inch circle, using Dough and Pizza Roller.

Step 2: Spread sauce evenly over dough.

Step 3: Add mozzarella, Parmesan, vegetables and meat. Bake 15 to 20 minutes or until crust is golden brown. Cut into wedges and serve.

Yield: 3 to 4 servings

Nonstick vegetable spray

1 box (21 to 24 ounces) brownie mix

½ cup chocolate chips

¼ cup butterscotch sauce

½ cup white chocolate chips

Vanilla ice cream

Chocolate sauce

Devilish Brownie Sundaes

Preheat oven to 350°F. Lightly spray 9" x 13" Baker with nonstick vegetable spray and set aside. In Classic 2-Qt. Batter Bowl, prepare brownie mix according to package directions, stirring in chocolate chips at end. Pour into prepared Baker and smooth top. Drizzle with butterscotch sauce. Using a table knife, cut back and forth through sauce to create swirled pattern. Sprinkle with white chocolate chips. Bake according to package directions. Let cool 10 minutes.

Cut brownies into 12 squares. Place a square on each of 4 plates. Top brownies with scoops of ice cream, drizzle with chocolate sauce and serve. Let remaining brownies cool completely; store at room temperature.

Yield: 4 servings

*The things you will **always** find in my kitchen (in addition to the basics on my "pantry list"): refrigerated bread products, assorted cheeses and vegetables—both fresh and frozen. Starting with these items I can prepare a wide variety of meals.*

South of the Border Supper

TURKEY ENCHILADA CASSEROLE • CONFETTI CORN SALAD
WATERMELON WEDGES • ICED TEA

*T**his is the perfect make-ahead meal to bring to a potluck. Using deli turkey (or some leftovers), put the enchilada casserole together the night before. Make the Confetti Corn Salad then, too; the longer it's chilled, the better it tastes.*

Grocery List

1 can (4 oz.) chopped mild green chilies
Ground cumin
8 oz. cooked turkey
1 bunch green onions
9 corn tortillas

2½ cups grated Cheddar cheese
5 cups frozen corn kernels
1 red bell pepper
1 green bell pepper
1 small red onion

Pantry Items

1 can (16 oz.) tomato sauce
Garlic
Chili powder
Dried oregano

Ground black pepper
Red wine vinegar
Brown sugar
Vegetable oil
Salt

1 can (16 ounces) tomato sauce

1 can (4 ounces) chopped mild green chilies, drained

1 garlic clove, crushed

1 tablespoon chili powder

2 teaspoons ground cumin

1 teaspoon dried oregano

¼ teaspoon ground black pepper

8 ounces cooked turkey, unsliced

1 bunch green onions

9 corn tortillas, cut in half

2½ cups grated Cheddar cheese

Turkey Enchilada Casserole

Preheat oven to 375°F. In 1-Quart Batter Bowl, combine tomato sauce, green chilies, garlic, chili powder, cumin, oregano and pepper. Using 5-inch Self-Sharpening Utility Knife, cut turkey into ½-inch cubes. Cut green onions into thin slices.

Line bottom of Deep Dish Baker with 6 tortilla halves. Spread a third of the sauce over tortillas. Cover tortillas with half the turkey and half the green onions and sprinkle with 1 cup of the cheese. Top with 6 more tortilla halves, half the remaining sauce, all the remaining turkey and green onions, and 1 more cup of the cheese. Top with remaining tortilla halves, remaining sauce and remaining ½ cup cheese. Bake 25 minutes. Let stand 5 minutes before serving.

Yield: 6 servings

5 cups frozen corn kernels, thawed

1 red bell pepper, cut into 1-inch-long strips

1 green bell pepper, cut into 1-inch-long strips

1 small red onion, chopped

¼ cup red wine vinegar

1 tablespoon brown sugar

2 tablespoons vegetable oil

½ teaspoon dried oregano

¼ teaspoon salt

Ground black pepper to taste

Confetti Corn Salad

In Classic 2-Qt. Batter Bowl, combine corn, bell peppers and onion. Stir with Bamboo Spoon to combine. In 1-Quart Batter Bowl, combine vinegar, brown sugar, oil, oregano, salt and pepper. Mix with Mini-Whipper. Pour dressing over corn mixture and mix well. Serve at room temperature or chilled.

Yield: 12 servings

Company for Dinner

Teriyaki Broil • Ginger Pilaf
Sunshine Kisses • Sparkling Water with Lemon

When you're entertaining guests in the middle of the week, here's an easy yet elegant menu you can partially prepare in advance, in case you get delayed at the office. If you make the cookies and marinate the steak the night before, you'll have plenty of time to broil the meat and vegetables, simmer the rice—and enjoy your guests.

Grocery List

1 bottle (10 oz.) teriyaki sauce
4 green onions
2 lbs. flank steak
1 pint mushrooms
1 pint cherry tomatoes
Butter
Fresh ginger

Rice
1 can (4 oz) mushroom stems and pieces
Frozen peas
1 package (18 to 19 oz) lemon cake mix
1 egg
Pecans

Pantry Items

Garlic
Honey
Chicken broth

Vegetable oil
Lemon
Powdered sugar

1 bottle (10 ounces) teriyaki sauce

2 green onions, sliced

1 garlic clove, pressed

1 tablespoon honey

2 pounds flank steak

1 pint mushrooms

1 pint cherry tomatoes

Teriyaki Broil

Combine teriyaki sauce, green onions, garlic and honey in Classic 2-Qt. Batter Bowl. Reserve ½ cup of the marinade and refrigerate. Place flank steak in a zip-top storage bag and pour remaining marinade over meat. Seal bag and refrigerate 4 hours or overnight.

Remove meat from marinade and place on broiler pan. Discard marinade in bag. Broil steak 4 inches from heat, turning once with Bar-B-Tongs and brushing other side with some of the reserved marinade, 8 to 10 minutes per side for medium-rare to medium. Meanwhile, thread mushrooms and tomatoes onto skewers. About 4 minutes before steak is done, brush vegetables with more of the remaining marinade and broil 4 minutes, turning once.

Cut steak across grain into thin slices, using Hold 'N Slice to secure meat while carving. Serve with skewered vegetables. Bring any remaining marinade to a boil and serve alongside steak.

Yield: 6 servings

Variation: Steak and vegetables may also be grilled. Grill steak over medium coals, turning several times, 17 to 21 minutes for medium-rare to medium. Grill vegetables 5 to 8 minutes.

2 tablespoons butter or margarine

1 tablespoon fresh ginger, peeled and finely chopped

1 cup long-grain white rice

1¾ cups chicken broth

1 can (4 ounces) mushroom stems and pieces, drained

2 green onions, thinly sliced

½ cup frozen peas

Ginger Pilaf

In 2-quart Generation II Saucepan, melt butter over medium heat. Add ginger and sauté 1 minute. Stir in rice, chicken broth, mushrooms and onions. Bring to a simmer. Cover and cook over very low heat 20 minutes. Remove from heat, add peas and stir. Cover and let stand 5 minutes. Fluff with a fork and serve.

Yield: 4 to 6 servings

1 package (18 to 19 ounces) lemon cake mix

1 egg, slightly beaten

⅓ cup vegetable oil

2 tablespoons water

⅓ cup pecans

Glaze:

1 lemon

½ cup powdered sugar

Sunshine Kisses

Preheat oven to 375°F. Combine cake mix, egg, oil and water in Classic 2-Qt. Batter Bowl. Stir until thoroughly combined (mixture will be dry). Chop pecans with Food Chopper; stir into dough. Using small Stainless Steel Scoop, drop dough 2 inches apart on Baking Stone. Bake 13 minutes or until lightly browned. Let cool 3 minutes. Then transfer to Non-Stick Cooling Rack.

Remove 1 teaspoon zest from lemon, using Lemon Zester/Scorer. Use Lemon Aid to remove 1 to 2 tablespoons juice from lemon. Whisk lemon zest, lemon juice and sugar in a small mixing bowl. Drizzle glaze on cooled cookies.

Yield: About 36 cookies

Hearty Soup and Salad

EXTRA EASY MINESTRONE • GREEN SALAD WITH ORANGE VINAIGRETTE
FRUIT-FILLED BAKED APPLES WITH WHIPPED CREAM

The Food Chopper and Garlic Press make short work of this chunky minestrone that tastes like it's been simmering for hours. Add some fruit and nuts to a green salad and baked apples, and you've got a satisfying and delicious meatless meal.

Grocery List

1 can (16 oz.) crushed tomatoes
1 can (15 oz.) navy or pinto beans
1 small onion
1 medium carrot
Frozen peas
Elbow macaroni
Slivered almonds
1 orange

1 bag (10 oz.) mixed salad greens
1 can (11 oz.) mandarin oranges
1 cup red grapes
Mixed dried fruit
Pecans
Butter
4 large Granny Smith apples
Whipped cream

Pantry Items

Beef broth
Dried basil
Garlic
Grated Parmesan cheese
Red wine vinegar
Honey
Dijon mustard

Salt
Ground black pepper
Vegetable oil
Light brown sugar
Ground cinnamon
Lemon juice

3 cups beef broth

1 cup water

1 can (16 ounces) crushed tomatoes

1 teaspoon dried basil

1 can (15 ounces) navy or pinto beans

1 small onion, chopped

1 medium carrot, chopped

2 garlic cloves, pressed

½ cup frozen peas

½ cup elbow macaroni

¼ cup grated Parmesan cheese

Extra Easy Minestrone

Place beef broth, water, tomatoes and basil in 4-quart Generation II Casserole. Bring to a boil over high heat. Meanwhile, drain beans, rinse under cold running water and drain well.

Chop onion and carrot with Food Chopper. Add onion, carrot, garlic, beans, peas and macaroni to boiling broth mixture. Return to a boil. Reduce heat to medium-low, cover and simmer, stirring occasionally, until macaroni is tender, about 10 minutes. Ladle into 4 bowls, sprinkle with cheese and serve.

Yield: 4 servings

½ cup slivered almonds

1 tablespoon red wine vinegar

1 tablespoon orange juice

1 tablespoon honey

1 teaspoon orange zest

1 teaspoon Dijon mustard

¼ teaspoon salt

Ground black pepper to taste

¼ cup vegetable oil

1 bag (10 ounces) mixed salad greens

1 can (11 ounces) mandarin oranges, well drained

1 cup red grapes, halved

Green Salad with Orange Vinaigrette

Preheat oven to 375°F. Spread almonds on 13-inch Round Baking Stone. Bake 7 to 9 minutes or until lightly toasted. Set aside to cool.*

In 1-Quart Batter Bowl, combine vinegar, orange juice, honey, orange zest, mustard, salt and pepper with Mini-Whipper. Slowly pour in oil, whisking with Mini-Whipper.

Combine salad greens, mandarin oranges, grapes and almonds in a salad bowl. Toss with orange vinaigrette and serve.

Yield: 4 servings

* For faster preparation, the toasting step
  may be eliminated.

¼ cup firmly packed light brown sugar

2 tablespoons diced mixed
   dried fruit or raisins

2 tablespoons chopped pecans

2 tablespoons butter or margarine,
   melted

½ teaspoon ground cinnamon

1½ teaspoons lemon juice

4 large Granny Smith apples

Whipped cream (optional)

Fruit-Filled Baked Apples with Whipped Cream

Preheat oven to 350°F. In small bowl, combine brown sugar, dried fruit, pecans, butter, cinnamon and ½ teaspoon of the lemon juice; mix well. Push Apple Corer into each apple from stem end without cutting through to bottom. Twist Corer and lift to remove partial core. Peel top inch of each apple. Rub remaining 1 teaspoon lemon juice over cut surfaces of apples to prevent browning.

Fill apples with fruit-nut mixture. Place in 8-inch Mini-Baker. Cover with Mini-Baking Bowl. Bake 35 to 40 minutes or until apples are tender when pierced with a knife. Serve warm topped with whipped cream, if desired.

Yield: 4 servings

Making the Fruit-Filled Baked Apples

1. Push Apple Corer into apple from stem end without cutting through to bottom. Twist Corer and lift to remove partial core.

2. Rub peeled part of each apple with lemon juice to prevent browning.

3. Place fruit and nut filled apples in bottom of Mini-Baker. Cover with Mini-Baking Bowl.

Speedy Ham and Spinach Risotto

Ham and Spinach Risotto • Bread Sticks • Simple Caesar Salad
Tropical Melon Slices • Sparkling Water with Lime

Leftover ham gets a new life in this one-dish meal that has it all: vegetable, grain, cheese and meat. While the risotto simmers, toss together an easy Caesar salad with crunchy romaine and croutons, and slice the melon for dessert.

Grocery List

1 medium onion
1 large red or yellow bell pepper
½ lb. cooked ham
Rice
1 package (10 oz.) frozen spinach
Romaine

Croutons
Caesar salad dressing
Coconut
Chopped almonds
½ cantaloupe
½ honeydew melon
2 limes

Pantry Items

Chicken broth
Ground black pepper

Grated Parmesan cheese
Lemon juice

1 medium onion

1 large red or yellow bell pepper

½ pound cooked ham, diced

1 cup rice

2 cups chicken broth

¼ teaspoon ground black pepper

1 package (10 ounces) frozen
    spinach, thawed and well drained

½ cup grated Parmesan cheese

Ham and Spinach Risotto

Coarsely chop onion and bell pepper with Food Chopper. Set aside separately.

In 10-inch Generation II Frying Pan, cook ham over medium-high heat 3 minutes. Add onion and cook until onion is soft, about 5 minutes. Add bell pepper and rice. Cook, stirring, until rice is coated with fat, about 1 minute. Add chicken broth and black pepper. Bring to a boil over medium-high heat. Reduce heat to low, cover and simmer 20 minutes. Add spinach, stirring until evenly distributed. Cover and cook 5 more minutes. Stir in cheese and serve.

Yield: 4 servings

1 small head romaine lettuce
    (about 8 cups torn pieces)

1 ounce Parmesan cheese
    (approximately ⅓ cup grated)

1 cup croutons

¼ cup Caesar salad dressing

1 tablespoon lemon juice

Ground black pepper to taste

Simple Caesar Salad

Wash lettuce, pat dry with a towel and tear into bite-size pieces. Put lettuce in a large serving bowl. Grate Parmesan cheese with Zyliss Cheese Grater. Add cheese, croutons, dressing and lemon juice. Using 3-Way Tongs, toss well. Season with pepper, toss again and serve.

Yield: 4 servings

¼ cup coconut

¼ cup chopped almonds

½ cantaloupe

½ honeydew melon

4 teaspoons lime juice

4 lime wedges

Tropical Melon Slices

Preheat oven to 350°F. Spread coconut and almonds on 13-inch Round Baking Stone. Bake, stirring occasionally, 7 to 8 minutes or until evenly browned. Set aside to cool.*

Using 5-inch Self-Sharpening Utility Knife, cut cantaloupe and honeydew into 8 thin wedges; then cut away rind. Arrange wedges on 4 plates. Drizzle lime juice over melon and sprinkle with coconut mixture. Add a lime wedge to each plate and serve.

Yield: 4 servings

* For faster preparation, the toasting step
  may be eliminated.

Crispy Chicken Dinner

CRISPY CHICKEN • CARROT-APPLE SALAD • CURLY CHEESE POTATOES
STRAWBERRY SHORTCAKE • MILK

I t's hard to say what the kids will love more: making the Curly Cheese Potatoes with the Apple Peeler/ Corer/Slicer, or eating them! You can coat the chicken as your little helpers turn potatoes into Slinkys, then pop both in a hot oven as you whip up the salad.

Grocery List

Cornflakes
Butter
1 broiler/fryer chicken
   (2 to 3 lbs.)
Milk
2 medium carrots

2 small apples
Orange juice
Romaine
4 medium potatoes
2 green onions

Pantry Items

Grated Parmesan cheese
Garlic
Dried thyme
Salt

Ground black pepper
Lemon juice
Sugar
Raisins

Crispy Chicken

2 cups cornflakes

¼ cup grated Parmesan cheese

2 tablespoons butter or margarine, melted

2 garlic cloves, pressed

1 teaspoon dried thyme

¼ teaspoon salt

¼ teaspoon ground black pepper

1 broiler/fryer chicken (2 to 3 pounds), cut up

¼ cup milk

Preheat oven to 400°F. Place cornflakes in a plastic storage bag. Roll Dough and Pizza Roller back and forth over bag until flakes are finely crushed. Place crushed flakes in Classic 2-Qt. Batter Bowl. Add cheese, butter, garlic, thyme, salt and pepper. Stir to combine.

Rinse chicken and pat dry. Place milk in 1-Quart Batter Bowl. Dip chicken pieces in milk and then roll in crumb mixture until well coated. Place chicken skin-side up in Deep Dish Baker. Press any remaining crumbs onto chicken pieces. Bake 40 to 50 minutes or until chicken is no longer pink in center. Serve hot.

Yield: 4 servings

Variation: Substitute 1½ pounds boneless chicken breasts for bone-in chicken. Bake 20 to 25 minutes or until chicken is no longer pink in center.

Carrot-Apple Salad

2 medium carrots

2 small apples, cored

2 tablespoons lemon juice

2 tablespoons orange juice

2 to 3 tablespoons sugar

½ cup raisins

4 romaine or red leaf lettuce leaves

Finely chop carrots and apples with Food Chopper and place in 1-Quart Batter Bowl. Add lemon juice, orange juice, sugar to taste and raisins. Stir to combine. Chill 20 minutes.

Place a lettuce leaf on each of 4 plates, add a scoop of salad and serve.

Yield: 4 servings

4 medium potatoes

¼ cup butter or margarine

1 garlic clove, pressed

⅓ cup grated Parmesan cheese

2 green onions, sliced

Curly Cheese Potatoes

Preheat oven to 400°F. Using Apple Peeler/Corer/Slicer, peel, core and slice potatoes to create long spirals. Slice "cores" into ¼-inch rounds. Place potatoes in Deep Dish Baker. Melt butter with garlic. Drizzle mixture over potatoes. Sprinkle with cheese and onions. Bake 35 to 45 minutes or until potatoes are lightly browned and tender. Serve warm.

Yield: 4 servings

Making the Curly Cheese Potatoes

1. Use the Apple Peeler/Corer/ Slicer to peel, core and slice the potatoes.

2. Slice cores into ¼-inch rounds with the 5-inch Self-Sharpening Utility Knife.

3. Sprinkle the potatoes with Parmesan cheese and green onions.

Tangy Taco Dinner

Taco Ring • Cucumber Salad • Double Chocolate Sundaes with
Homemade Fudge Sauce • Lemonade

For a change of pace, serve your tacos in an easy yet impressive crescent-roll ring that bakes while you prepare the Cucumber Salad. Then use the Covered Micro-Cooker to make quick work of melting the to-die-for fudge sauce. No more burnt chocolate!

Grocery List

½ lb. ground beef
1 package (1.25 oz.) taco
  seasoning mix
1 cup shredded Cheddar
  cheese
2 packages (8oz. each)
  refrigerated crescent
  roll dough
1 medium green bell
  pepper
Lettuce
1 medium tomato
1 small onion

Pitted black olives
Sour cream
Plain yogurt
Fresh mint
Fresh dill
2 medium cucumbers
Milk chocolate chips
Butter
1 can (5 oz.)
  evaporated milk
Chocolate ice cream
Whipped cream

Pantry Items

Salsa
Cider vinegar
Sugar

Salt
Ground black pepper

½ pound ground beef, cooked and drained

1 package (1.25 ounces) taco seasoning mix

1 cup shredded Cheddar cheese

2 tablespoons water

2 packages (8 ounces each) refrigerated crescent roll dough

1 medium green bell pepper

½ head lettuce

1 medium tomato

1 small onion

½ cup whole pitted black olives

1 cup salsa

Sour cream

Taco Ring

Preheat oven to 375°F. Combine meat, seasoning mix, cheese and water in Classic 2-Qt. Batter Bowl. Arrange crescent triangles in a circle on 13-inch Round Baking Stone, with bases overlapping in center and points to outside (there should be a 5-inch-diameter circle in center). Using medium Stainless Steel Scoop, spoon meat mixture over rolls. Fold points of triangles over filling and tuck under base at center (filling will not be completely covered). Bake 20 to 25 minutes or until golden brown.

Using V-Shaped Cutter, cut off the top of bell pepper. Shred lettuce and cube tomato with 5-inch Self-Sharpening Utility Knife. Chop onion with Food Chopper. Slice olives, using Egg Slicer. Place bell pepper in center of ring; fill with salsa. Mound lettuce, onion, tomato and olives around pepper. Using Easy Accent Decorator, garnish with sour cream. Cut with Pizza Cutter and serve with Mini-Serving Spatula.

Yield: 8 servings

Making the Taco Ring

1. Arrange crescent triangles in a circle on the 13-inch Round Baking Stone, with bases overlapping in center and points to the outside.

2. Scoop meat mixture over crescent rolls with medium Stainless Steel Scoop.

3. Fold points of triangles over filling and tuck under base at center.

½ cup plain yogurt

½ cup sour cream

1 tablespoon cider vinegar

1 tablespoon sugar

2 tablespoons minced fresh mint

2 teaspoons minced fresh dill

2 medium cucumbers

Salt and ground black pepper to taste

Cucumber Salad

In Classic 2-Qt. Batter Bowl, combine yogurt, sour cream, vinegar and sugar. Using Kitchen Cutters, finely mince mint and dill. Add to yogurt mixture. Peel cucumbers, using Vegetable Peeler. Place Vario-Slicer over Batter Bowl and thinly slice cucumbers into yogurt mixture. Season with salt and pepper. Stir to combine. Chill slightly before serving.

Yield: 4 to 6 servings

Sauce:

1½ cups milk chocolate chips

2 tablespoons butter or margarine

1 can (5 ounces) evaporated milk

Sundaes:

Chocolate ice cream

Whipped cream

Double Chocolate Sundaes with Homemade Fudge Sauce

Place chocolate chips and butter in Micro-Cooker and microwave on High 1 minute. Stir with 10-inch Whisk. Microwave 1 more minute. Add evaporated milk and combine with Whisk. Microwave 1 more minute. Whisk until smooth. Microwave 1 to 2 more minutes or until glossy and thick. Set aside briefly. (Sauce will thicken as it sits.)

Scoop chocolate ice cream into bowls or sundae glasses. Top with warm fudge sauce and a dollop of whipped cream. Serve immediately.

Yield: 2 cups fudge sauce

Ravioli on the Run

RAVIOLI CARBONARA • SUPER-QUICK GARLIC BREAD • STEAMED BROCCOLI
FRESH CHERRIES AND GRAPES • CLUB SODA AND JUICE

With frozen ravioli and dairy-aisle Alfredo sauce, your next pasta night will seem sophisticated (but couldn't be simpler). As the ravioli boils and the broccoli steams, warm the bread and jazz up the Alfredo sauce with some bacon, cream and basil.

Grocery List

Bacon
Refrigerated Alfredo sauce
Milk
Fresh basil

1 lb. frozen or refrigerated ravioli
1 (10 to 12 oz.) loaf Italian Bread
Butter

Pantry Items

Ground black pepper
Garlic

Salt

Ravioli Carbonara

8 slices bacon, diced

1 cup refrigerated Alfredo sauce

¼ cup milk

¼ cup chopped fresh basil or
    1 tablespoon dried basil

1 pound frozen or refrigerated ravioli

Ground black pepper to taste

Fill 4-quart Generation II Casserole with water, cover and bring to a boil. Meanwhile, sauté bacon in 2-quart Generation II Saucepan until crisp. Drain off fat. Stir in Alfredo sauce, milk and basil. Set aside.

Cook ravioli, uncovered, in boiling water according to package directions. Drain and return to Casserole. Pour sauce over ravioli and stir gently. Warm over low heat, season with pepper and serve.

Yield: 4 servings

Super-Quick Garlic Bread

1 loaf Italian bread (10 to
    12 ounces)

½ cup butter or margarine

2 garlic cloves, pressed

¼ teaspoon salt

1 tablespoon minced fresh basil or
    1 teaspoon dried basil

Preheat oven to 375°F. Using Serrated Bread Knife, cut bread into 1-inch-thick slices. Place bread slices on 13-inch Round Baking Stone.

Place butter in Covered Micro-Cooker. Microwave on High 1 minute or just until a small lump of unmelted butter remains. Add garlic, salt and basil to butter. Mix with Pastry Brush. Brush butter mixture on both sides of bread slices. Bake 13 to 15 minutes or until bread is crisp around edges. Serve hot.

Yield: 4 to 6 servings

When I'm cooking pasta, I make enough to use twice: once with a hot sauce as a main dish or side dish, and later in a salad with cut-up meat or vegetables.

Pineapple Ham Steak

PINEAPPLE HAM STEAK • EASY CHEESY BISCUITS • PRALINE SQUASH
SORBET • APPLE JUICE

The kids will love making the Easy Cheesy
Biscuits with the Cut-N-Seal while you sizzle
the ham steak and prepare the Praline Squash.
With a brown sugar and pecan topping, this
vegetable almost seems like dessert!

Pineapple Ham Steak

2 cans (8¼ ounces each) unsweetened juice-packed pineapple rings

2 tablespoons dried mustard

1 tablespoon brown sugar

¼ teaspoon ground cloves

⅛ teaspoon ground black pepper

1½-pound cooked ham steak

Drain pineapple, reserving ¼ cup of the juice. Combine reserved juice, mustard, brown sugar, cloves and pepper in 1-Quart Batter Bowl. Place ham steak in 12-inch Generation II Family Skillet and brush top with half of the glaze. Cook over medium-high heat until lightly browned, about 4 minutes. Turn ham steak over and brush with remaining glaze. Top with pineapple rings. Cover and cook until ham and pineapple rings are heated through, 4 to 7 more minutes. Serve warm.

Yield: 4 servings

Easy Cheesy Biscuits

1 package (12 ounces) refrigerated flaky biscuits

½ cup grated Cheddar cheese

2 tablespoons water

1 tablespoon grated Parmesan cheese

Preheat oven to 400°F. Place biscuits on 13-inch or 15-inch Round Baking Stone. Split each biscuit in half horizontally. Sprinkle Cheddar cheese on bottom half of each biscuit. Replace tops and flatten slightly with palm of your hand. Place 3-inch Cut-N-Seal over each biscuit and push handle to seal and crimp edges. Brush tops of biscuits with water, using Pastry Brush. Sprinkle with Parmesan cheese. Bake 14 to 16 minutes or until tops and bottoms of biscuits are browned. Serve warm.

Yield: 10 biscuits

Praline Squash

2 medium acorn squash

¼ cup chopped pecans

¼ cup firmly packed brown sugar

¼ teaspoon ground cinnamon

2 tablespoons butter or margarine

Cut squash in half and remove strings and seeds. Place squash cut-side down in Deep Dish Baker. Microwave on High 15 to 17 minutes or until tender. Let stand 5 minutes. Meanwhile, coarsely chop pecans with Food Chopper. Combine pecans, brown sugar and cinnamon in 1-Quart Batter Bowl.

Turn squash cut-side up and gently mash insides, leaving shells intact. Dot each half with butter and sprinkle with brown sugar mixture. Microwave 2 minutes or until brown sugar is melted. Serve hot.

Yield: 4 servings

Chicken Parmesan Dinner

CHICKEN PARMESAN • STEAMED SNOW PEAS • BAKED POTATO • POUND CAKE WITH PEACHES
AND RASPBERRY SAUCE • SPARKLING WATER WITH A SPLASH OF ORANGE JUICE

O*nce you've got the potatoes and chicken baking, you can quickly pull together the raspberry dessert sauce. By the time you've finished with the main course, the sauce will be cool enough to pour over pound cake and peaches—a lovely, classic dessert.*

Grocery List

2 eggs
4 boneless, skinless chick-
    en breast halves
    (about 1 lb.)
4 slices mozzarella cheese
Pizza sauce

1 package (10 oz.) frozen
    raspberries in light
    syrup
8 slices pound cake
1 can (16 oz.) sliced
    cling peaches

Pantry Items

Garlic
Bread crumbs
Grated Parmesan cheese
Italian seasoning

Salt
Olive oil
Sugar
Cornstarch

2 egg whites

1 tablespoon water

1 large garlic clove

½ cup bread crumbs

¼ cup grated Parmesan cheese

1½ teaspoons Italian seasoning

¼ teaspoon salt

4 boneless, skinless chicken breast
   halves (about 1 pound total)

1 tablespoon olive oil, divided

4 slices mozzarella cheese

½ cup pizza sauce, warmed

Chicken Parmesan

In 1-Quart Batter Bowl, beat egg whites and water with 10-inch Whisk until foamy. Crush garlic with Garlic Press and add to egg whites. On a plate, combine bread crumbs, Parmesan, Italian seasoning and salt. Dip chicken pieces into egg whites and then into crumb mixture. Shake off excess crumbs. Dip each piece again into egg whites and crumb mixture.

Heat half of the oil in 10-inch Generation II Frying Pan over medium-high heat. Add chicken and cook until golden brown, about 4 minutes. Add remaining oil and turn chicken over. Cook until chicken is no longer pink in center, about 4 more minutes. Place a slice of mozzarella on each piece of chicken. Reduce heat to low, cover and cook until cheese is melted, 2 to 3 more minutes. Transfer chicken to a serving plate and drizzle with pizza sauce. Serve hot.

Yield: 4 servings

No one likes leftovers a day or two after—but they won't mind them a week or two later, served with a salad and maybe some fresh vegetables! I freeze all my leftovers, mark them well and pull them out at the beginning of a particularly hectic day. Even if I'm working late, I know we'll have a satisfying meal that night.

1 package (10 ounces) frozen raspberries in light syrup, thawed

1 tablespoon sugar

1 tablespoon cornstarch

8 slices* (each ½ inch thick) pound cake, purchased or homemade

1 can (16 ounces) sliced cling peaches, drained

Pound Cake with Peaches and Raspberry Sauce

Combine raspberries, sugar and cornstarch in 1½-quart Generation II Saucepan. Stir with Bamboo Spoon. Bring to a boil over medium heat; then set aside to cool.

Place 2 slices of the pound cake on each of 4 dessert plates. Top cake slices with peaches, spoon raspberry sauce over peaches and serve.

Yield: 4 servings

* For a decorative edge, slice pound cake with Garnisher.

Supper from the Sea

BAKED ORANGE ROUGHY WITH LEMON SAUCE • BROCCOLI-CHEDDAR GRATIN
STEAMED RED POTATOES WITH DILL • COOKIES • ICED TEA

While the broccoli and potatoes are steaming, make the cheesy-crumb topping for the gratin and the lemon sauce for the fish. Bake both for about 10 minutes, toss some butter and dill into the new potatoes—and serve!

Grocery List

1¼ to 1½ lbs. orange roughy fillets
Broccoli
Butter

1 cup shredded Cheddar cheese
2 lbs. very small red potatoes
Fresh dill

Pantry Items

Lemon
Mayonnaise
Parsley
Salt

Ground black pepper
Bread crumbs
Dried oregano

Baked Orange Roughy with Lemon Sauce

1 lemon

½ cup mayonnaise

2 tablespoons parsley, finely snipped

¼ teaspoon salt

¼ teaspoon ground black pepper

1¼ to 1½ pounds orange roughy fillets

Preheat oven to 450°F. Scrape Lemon Zester/Scorer across lemon to make 1 tablespoon zest. Use Lemon Aid to remove 2 tablespoons juice from lemon. In 1-Quart Batter Bowl, combine lemon juice, lemon zest, mayonnaise, parsley, salt and pepper. Place orange roughy in Deep Dish Baker. Spread fillets with half the lemon mixture. Bake 10 to 12 minutes or until fish flakes easily with a fork. Serve remaining lemon sauce alongside fish.

Yield: 4 servings

Broccoli-Cheddar Gratin

3 large stalks broccoli

½ cup unseasoned bread crumbs

½ teaspoon dried oregano

¼ teaspoon salt

¼ teaspoon ground black pepper

3 tablespoons butter or margarine, melted

1 cup shredded Cheddar cheese

Preheat oven to 450°F. Cut broccoli into florets and place in Generation II Stainless Steel Steamer. Fill 2-quart Generation II Saucepan with water and bring to a boil. Place steamer over boiling water and cover. Steam broccoli just until tender, 10 to 12 minutes. Meanwhile, combine bread crumbs, oregano, salt and pepper in 1-Quart Batter Bowl. Stir in butter and cheese.

Place broccoli in Deep Dish Baker. Sprinkle crumb mixture over broccoli. Bake 5 to 7 minutes or just until cheese begins to melt. Serve hot.

Yield: 6 servings

Steamed Red Potatoes with Dill

2 pounds very small red potatoes

2 tablespoons butter or margarine

2 tablespoons chopped fresh dill

½ teaspoon salt

⅛ teaspoon ground black pepper

Wash and scrub potatoes and place in Generation II Stainless Steel Steamer. Fill 4-quart Generation II Saucepan with water and bring to a boil. Place steamer over boiling water and cover. Steam potatoes until tender, 14 to 16 minutes. Transfer to a serving bowl. Toss with butter, dill, salt and pepper and serve.

Yield: 4 to 6 servings

Oriental Delight

EGG FOO YUNG • WHITE RICE • SPINACH SALAD WITH
ORIENTAL DRESSING • ALMOND COOKIES • HOT TEA

Now you can quickly make one of your favorite
takeout dinners at home, with fresh ingredients
and without the worry about MSG or artificial
ingredients. Round out the meal with a nutritious
spinach salad tossed in an easy sesame dressing.

Grocery List

7 eggs
½ cup cooked ham
1 green bell pepper
½ cup bean sprouts
1 green onion
10 oz. spinach

1 cup cherry tomatoes
1 red bell pepper
½ cup water chestnuts
Sesame seeds
Fresh ginger
Butter

Pantry Items

Salt
Ground black pepper
Vegetable oil
Lemons
Soy sauce

Garlic
Sugar
Almond extract
All-purpose flour
Baking powder

6 eggs, slightly beaten

½ cup diced cooked ham

½ green bell pepper, seeded and diced

½ cup bean sprouts

1 thinly sliced green onion (including top)

½ teaspoon salt

¼ teaspoon ground black pepper

2 teaspoons vegetable oil

Egg Foo Yung

Combine eggs, ham, bell pepper, bean sprouts, onion, salt and pepper in Classic 2-Qt. Batter Bowl. Heat 1 teaspoon of the oil on 11-inch Generation II Square Griddle over medium-high heat. Pour half the egg mixture onto griddle. As edge begins to set, lift with spatula and tilt griddle to let uncooked egg flow underneath. When eggs no longer flow freely, run a spatula around edge, fold in half and slide onto a warm serving plate. Cover loosely to keep warm. Heat remaining 1 teaspoon oil and repeat to cook remaining egg mixture. Serve immediately.

Yield: 4 servings

10 ounces spinach, washed, trimmed and dried

1 cup cherry tomatoes, halved

½ red bell pepper, cut into thin strips

¼ cup sliced water chestnuts

Oriental Dressing:

3 tablespoons vegetable oil

1 tablespoon lemon juice

1 tablespoon sesame seeds, toasted*

1½ teaspoons soy sauce

1 garlic clove, pressed

½ teaspoon fresh ginger, finely chopped with Food Chopper

Salt and ground black pepper to taste

Spinach Salad with Oriental Dressing

Combine spinach, tomatoes, red pepper and water chestnuts in a salad bowl. In 1-Quart Batter Bowl, combine oil, lemon juice, sesame seeds, soy sauce, garlic, ginger, salt and pepper. Beat with Mini-Whipper until combined. Pour over salad, toss and serve.

Yield: 4 servings

* To toast sesame seeds, place seeds in 8-inch Generation II Open Sauté Pan. Cook over medium heat, stirring often, until golden brown.

For a quick stir-fry, stop at the salad bar of your favorite grocery store and pick up a quarter-pound of cut-up vegetables. A great timesaver!

1 cup sugar

¾ cup butter or margarine

1 egg, slightly beaten

1 teaspoon almond extract

1½ cups all-purpose flour

1 teaspoon baking powder

Almond Cookies

Preheat oven to 375°F. In mixer bowl, cream sugar and butter on high speed until light and fluffy. Add egg and almond extract and continue to beat until well blended. On low speed, add flour and baking powder and mix until combined. Using Small Stainless Steel Scoop, drop dough 2 inches apart on 15-inch Round Baking Stone. Bake 11 to 13 minutes or until edges are lightly browned.

Yield: About 36 cookies

Meat 'n' Potato Salad Dinner

MEAT 'N' POTATO SALAD • PICKLES AND OLIVES • CARROT STICKS
EASY APPLE PIE TARTS • FRUIT PUNCH

You and the kids can work side by side: For the warm salad, toss the meat and potatoes in the same Batter Bowl in which you mixed the dressing, while your children have a ball making the easy dessert tarts with the Cut-N-Seal.

Grocery List

1 lb. smoked sausage
1 lb. small red potatoes
Sour cream
1 large green bell pepper
1 medium red onion

1 can (21 oz.) apple pie filling
Fresh bread slices or pie crust dough
Butter

Pantry Items

Chicken broth
Cider vinegar
Mayonnaise
Dijon mustard

Sugar
Salt
Ground cinnamon

Meat 'n' Potato Salad

1 pound smoked sausage,
    cut into ½-inch-thick slices

1 pound small red potatoes,
    cut into ½-inch cubes

1½ cups chicken broth

½ cup sour cream

2 tablespoons cider vinegar

2 tablespoons mayonnaise

2 teaspoons Dijon mustard

1 teaspoon sugar

½ teaspoon salt

1 large green bell pepper, diced

½ cup red onion chopped
    with Food Chopper

Place sausage, potatoes and chicken broth in 10-inch Generation II Frying Pan. Bring to a boil over medium-high heat. Reduce to a simmer, cover and cook until potatoes are tender, about 10 minutes. Meanwhile, combine sour cream, vinegar, mayonnaise, mustard, sugar and salt in Classic 2-Qt. Batter Bowl.

When sausage and potatoes are finished cooking, drain and let cool slightly, about 5 minutes. Add sausage, potatoes, bell pepper and onion to Batter Bowl and toss to coat. Serve warm.

Yield: 4 servings

Easy Apple Pie Tarts

1 can (21 ounces) apple pie filling

Fresh bread slices or
    pie crust dough

½ cup butter or margarine,
    melted

½ cup sugar

½ teaspoon ground cinnamon

Preheat oven to 375°F. Run a knife through pie filling to coarsely chop apples. Place 1 tablespoon of the pie filling in center of a bread slice. Top with another bread slice. Repeat until all filling is used. Use 3-inch Cut-N-Seal to cut and seal tarts. Lightly brush both sides of tarts with butter. Combine sugar and cinnamon in Flour/Sugar Shaker. Sprinkle over tarts. Place on Baking Stone. Bake 15 minutes or until lightly browned.

Yield: 32 tarts*

* If time is short, cut recipe in half. Pie filling can be stored
  in the refrigerator after opening.

A Light Italian Supper

TORTELLINI SALAD WITH GARDEN VEGETABLES • SLICED TOMATOES AND MOZZARELLA WITH BASIL
BREADSTICKS • CARROT CAKE COOKIES • ICED TEA

A tasty salad of pasta and crunchy fresh vegetables will brighten your table with natural color from the garden. Sneak some veggies into dessert, too, which you can make while the tortellini is cooking. Just add grated fresh carrot, walnuts and cinnamon to spice cake mix for delicious carrot cake cookies.

Grocery List

1 lb. frozen or refrigerated tortellini
1 yellow or red bell pepper
1 small zucchini
Frozen peas
1 small red onion
Creamy Italian salad dressing

2 large ripe tomatoes
6 oz. fresh mozzarella cheese
Italian dressing
Fresh basil
1 package (18 to 19 oz.) spice cake mix
1 egg
2 medium carrots
Walnuts

Pantry Items

Ground black pepper
Vegetable oil

Ground cinnamon
Powdered sugar

1 pound frozen or refrigerated
  tortellini

½ yellow or red bell pepper, diced

1 small zucchini, cut into thin sticks

1 cup frozen peas, thawed

½ small red onion, chopped
  with Food Chopper

¾ cup creamy Italian salad dressing

Tortellini Salad with Garden Vegetables

Cook tortellini according to package directions just until tender. Drain, rinse under cold running water and drain again. Transfer to Classic 2-Qt. Batter Bowl. Cut bell pepper and zucchini as indicated with 5-inch Self-Sharpening Utility Knife. Add remaining ingredients and toss well with 3-Way Tongs. Serve at room temperature or chilled.

Yield: 4 servings

2 large, ripe tomatoes

6 ounces fresh mozzarella cheese,*
  thinly sliced

1 tablespoon Italian dressing

2 tablespoons thinly sliced
  fresh basil **

Ground black pepper to taste

Whole basil leaves for garnish
  (optional)

Sliced Tomatoes and Mozzarella with Basil

Using Vario-Slicer, thinly slice tomatoes. Arrange tomatoes and mozzarella in overlapping rows on a platter. Drizzle with dressing. Sprinkle with sliced basil and pepper. Garnish with whole basil leaves, if desired, and serve.

Yield: 4 servings

* Fresh mozzarella is a soft-textured cheese that is
  packed in liquid and sold in the deli section of grocery
  stores or in Italian specialty stores. If desired,
  substitute 4 ounces regular mozzarella.

** For quick and even slices, stack basil leaves on top
  of each other, then roll stack of leaves into a "log."
  Slice thinly with 3-inch Self-Sharpening Paring Knife.

1 package (18 to 19 ounces) spice cake mix

1 egg, slightly beaten

⅓ cup vegetable oil

¼ cup water

½ teaspoon ground cinnamon

2 medium carrots, peeled

½ cup walnuts

Powdered sugar

Carrot Cake Cookies

Preheat oven to 350°F. Place cake mix, egg, oil, water and cinnamon in Classic 2-Qt. Batter Bowl. Combine with Mix 'N Scraper. Grate carrots with Grater-Slicer (you should have about ½ cup) and add to cake mixture. Chop walnuts with Food Chopper and stir into mixture. Using small Stainless Steel Scoop, drop dough 2 inches apart on 15-inch Round Baking Stone. Bake 18 to 20 minutes or until lightly browned. Let cool 3 minutes. Using Mini-Serving Spatula, transfer cookies to Non-Stick Cooling Rack. Place powdered sugar in Flour/Sugar Shaker and sprinkle over cooled cookies.

Yield: About 36 cookies

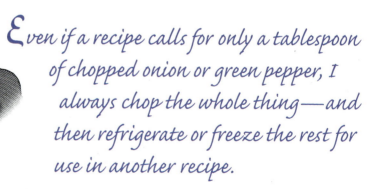

Even if a recipe calls for only a tablespoon of chopped onion or green pepper, I always chop the whole thing—and then refrigerate or freeze the rest for use in another recipe.

Down-Home Barbecue

MIDWINTER BBQ CHICKEN • SWEET HOME FRIES • DOUBLE CORN STICKS
FRESH PINEAPPLE AND STRAWBERRIES • MILK

When you crave the flavors of summer, try this meal any time of the year: moist, barbecued chicken (salsa's the secret ingredient!), crinkle-cut sweet potato fries (made with the Garnisher) and cheesy corn sticks that the kids will love creating (and eating).

Grocery List

4 large boneless, skinless chicken breast halves (about 1 1/2 lbs.)
2 medium sweet potatoes
Honey Dijon barbecue sauce
Sour cream

1 package (11.5 oz.) refrigerated corn bread twists
1/2 cup canned corn
1/2 cup grated Monterey Jack cheese

Pantry Items

Salsa
Ketchup
Brown sugar
Worcestershire sauce

Olive oil
Salt
Ground black pepper

¾ cup mild salsa, well drained

¾ cup ketchup

¼ cup firmly packed brown sugar

1 tablespoon Worcestershire sauce

4 large boneless, skinless chicken breast halves (about 1½ pounds total)

Midwinter BBQ Chicken

Preheat oven to 400°F. In Classsic 2-Qt. Batter Bowl, combine salsa, ketchup, brown sugar and Worcestershire sauce. Add chicken breasts and toss to coat well. Place chicken in Deep Dish Baker and pour excess sauce over top. Bake, uncovered, 30 minutes or until chicken is no longer pink in center. Serve hot.

Yield: 4 servings

2 medium sweet potatoes

½ teaspoon olive oil

Salt and ground black pepper to taste

Dip:

½ cup honey Dijon barbecue sauce

½ cup sour cream

Sweet Home Fries

Preheat oven to 400°F. Peel potatoes with Vegetable Peeler. Slice potatoes in half lengthwise and then quarter, using Garnisher. Continue to slice potatoes into fries. Place in Classsic 2-Qt. Batter Bowl, add oil and toss to coat. Place on 13-inch Round Baking Stone and bake 20 to 25 minutes or until tender and slightly crisp. Meanwhile, combine barbecue sauce and sour cream, using 10-inch Whisk. Refrigerate. Season fries with salt and pepper and serve with dip.

Yield: 4 to 6 servings

1 package (11.5 ounces) refrigerated corn bread twists

½ cup canned corn, drained

½ cup grated Monterey Jack cheese

Double Corn Sticks

Preheat oven to 350°F. Place a piece of Kitchen Parchment on 13-inch Round Baking Stone. Unroll 8 of the corn bread twists but do not separate. Place twists on paper and, using Dough and Pizza Roller, roll into a 7-inch square. Sprinkle corn and cheese over the dough. Roll remaining twists into a 7-inch square on another piece of Kitchen Parchment. Lay second piece of dough over the first.

Cut dough into 8 sticks, using Pizza Cutter, but do not separate. Bake 15 minutes. Cut between sticks again with Pizza Cutter and separate sticks slightly, leaving about ½ inch between each stick. Return to oven and bake 7 to 10 more minutes or until golden brown. Serve warm or at room temperature.

Yield: 8 sticks

Making the Double Corn Sticks

1. On the Round Baking Stone, use the Dough and Pizza Roller to flatten 8 of the corn bread twists into a square.

2. Sprinkle the dough with corn and cheese. Roll the remaining twists into a square.

3. Lay the second piece of dough over the corn and cheese.

4. Use the Pizza Cutter to cut the dough into 8 sticks.

BREAKFASTS LUNCHES AND SNACKS

So many of us fall into the rut of making the same old thing, day after day. But with a few quiet moments of menu-planning once a week or so, as well as these new ideas for quick breakfasts, lunches and snacks, your mealtimes will be not only delicious but interesting, too!

An American Classic

SCRAMBLED EGGS WITH SWISS CHEESE • BACON
GLAZED PEACH COFFEECAKE • CRANBERRY JUICE

With a can of peaches and some peach or apricot preserves, you can easily make everyday coffeecake something special. As it bakes, prepare the bacon in the microwave, and your hands will be free to scramble the eggs on the stovetop.

Grocery List

2 cups baking and
   biscuit mix
Milk
2 eggs

Butter
1 can (16 oz.) sliced
   yellow cling peaches
Peach or apricot preserves

Pantry Items

Nonstick vegetable spray
Sugar

Almond extract
Lemon

2 cups baking and biscuit mix

½ cup milk

¼ cup sugar

2 eggs

2 tablespoons butter or
    margarine, melted

1 teaspoon almond extract

1 teaspoon lemon zest

1 can (16 ounces) sliced yellow
    cling peaches, drained

3 tablespoons peach or apricot
    preserves

Glazed Peach Coffeecake

Preheat oven to 375°F. Lightly spray Deep Dish Baker with nonstick vegetable spray. Set aside.

Place baking mix, milk, sugar, eggs, butter, almond extract and lemon zest in Classic 2-Qt. Batter Bowl. Combine with 10-inch Whisk just until dry ingredients are no longer visible. Pour batter into prepared Baker and spread evenly with Super Scraper. Arrange peach slices in a spokelike pattern over top of batter, placing 2 or 3 slices in center. Bake 20 minutes or until Cake Tester inserted in center comes out clean.

Place preserves in Micro-Cooker. Microwave on High 25 seconds. Brush preserves over top of cake with Pastry Brush. Let cool 10 minutes before serving.

Yield: 6 to 8 servings

Sunday Brunch

CHEESY POTATO PIE • MELON WEDGES
TOASTED WHOLE WHEAT BREAD WITH JAM • ORANGE JUICE

Frozen hash browns, stir-fried with onion, are mixed with cheese and eggs in this hearty pie topped with crumbled bacon—the perfect, rib-sticking dish to serve when your stomach says breakfast but the clock says lunch.

Grocery List

1 medium onion
4 cups frozen Southern-
    style hash brown
    potatoes
6 eggs
Milk

Parsley
1 cup grated Cheddar
    cheese
Real bacon bits

Pantry Items

Vegetable oil
Salt

Ground black pepper

1 medium onion

2 tablespoons vegetable oil

4 cups frozen Southern-style hash
    brown potatoes (about half a
    32-ounce bag)

6 eggs

¼ cup milk

2 tablespoons chopped parsley

½ teaspoon salt

¼ teaspoon ground black pepper

1 cup grated Cheddar cheese

2 tablespoons real bacon bits

Cheesy Potato Pie

Preheat oven to 350°F. Coarsely chop onion with Food Chopper.
Heat oil in 10-inch Generation II Frying Pan over medium-high
heat. Add onion and frozen potatoes to pan. Cook over medium-
high heat, stirring occasionally, until lightly browned, about
10 minutes. Meanwhile, beat eggs with milk, parsley, salt and
pepper in 1-Quart Batter Bowl. Stir in cheese.

Pour egg mixture over potatoes and stir gently. Sprinkle bacon
bits on top. Place skillet in oven and bake 12 to 14 minutes or
until eggs are set. Cut into wedges with Bamboo Spatula and serve.

Yield: 6 servings

*Whether it's breakfast, lunch or dinner, meal prepa-
ration doesn't have to be a solitary chore; in fact it
can be a wonderful opportunity for quality family
time together. Invite your children—and your
spouse—to help make sandwiches, chop vegetables or assemble the
main dish as you all chat leisurely about what's happening in your
individual lives. Instead of dreading that mealtime scramble, you
just might end up loving it!*

Griddle Cakes and Sausage

GRIDDLE CAKES WITH STRAWBERRY-ORANGE SAUCE • SAUSAGE
FLUTED GRAPEFRUIT HALVES • MILK

Weekend guests will feel like they're staying in a country inn when you serve Sunday morning pancakes with this easy strawberry-orange sauce, rather than syrup. Sausage and Fluted Grapefuit Halves round out this welcoming meal.

Grocery List

1 package (10 oz) frozen sliced strawberries with sugar
Orange juice concentrate

3 eggs
1 cup cottage cheese
Butter

Pantry Items

Lemon
All-purpose flour
Sugar

Salt
Vegetable oil

1 package (10 ounces) frozen sliced strawberries with sugar, thawed

2 tablespoons frozen orange juice concentrate

1 tablespoon lemon juice

½ teaspoon lemon zest

3 eggs

1 cup cottage cheese

¼ cup all-purpose flour

1 tablespoon sugar

1 tablespoon butter or margarine, melted

Pinch of salt

About 1 tablespoon vegetable oil

Griddle Cakes with Strawberry-Orange Sauce

Place strawberries, orange juice, lemon juice and lemon zest in Classic 2-Qt. Batter Bowl. Using Pastry Blender, mash berries. Set aside.

In 1-Quart Batter Bowl, beat eggs and cottage cheese with 10-inch Whisk until well mixed, leaving cottage cheese slightly lumpy for texture. Add flour, sugar, melted butter and salt to egg mixture. Mix well with 10-inch Whisk.

Lightly oil 11-inch Generation II Square Griddle and place over medium-high heat until hot but not smoking. For each pancake, pour a scant ¼ cup of the batter onto griddle. Cook until bubbles form and top of pancake looks dry, 2 to 3 minutes. Turn pancake over and cook until bottom is nicely browned, about 1 more minute. Serve pancakes with strawberry-orange sauce.

Yield: 8 pancakes

I consider the microwave as an extension of my rangetop. I use it for everything that I used to do on the top of the stove—steaming vegetables, melting butter or chocolate, cooking rice—but in half the time. And no more burned pots! With the microwave timer, you always know when it's done.

Breakfast with a Twist

GOOEY CARAMEL ROLLS • TANGY FRUIT SALAD WITH SWEET YOGURT DRESSING
EXTRA SPECIAL HOT CHOCOLATE

As the caramel rolls bake, mix together this healthy breakfast salad of pineapple, blueberries, strawberries and melon balls (the Small Stainless Steel Scoop makes them the perfect size). A fresh strawberry dressing adds just the right, light touch.

64

¾ cup pecans

1¼ cups firmly packed brown sugar

½ cup butter or margarine, melted

¼ cup light corn syrup

1 tablespoon ground cinnamon

2 cans (7.5 ounces each) refrigerated buttermilk biscuits

Gooey Caramel Rolls

Preheat oven to 375°F. Chop pecans with Food Chopper. Combine nuts, brown sugar, butter, corn syrup and cinnamon in 1-Quart Batter Bowl. Mix well. Using Dough and Pizza Roller, roll 1 can of biscuits into a 6- by 12-inch rectangle. Spread ½ cup of the filling over dough; roll up lengthwise. Using Serrated Bread Knife, cut into 12 slices, each 1 inch thick. Repeat with second can of biscuits and ½ cup more filling. Place rolls ½ inch apart in Deep Dish Baker. Top with remaining filling. Bake 25 to 30 minutes. Serve warm.

Yield: 24 rolls

Making the Gooey Caramel Rolls

1. Lay 10 biscuits out on a clean surface and use the Dough and Pizza Roller to roll them into a 6- by 12-inch rectangle.

2. Spread ½ cup filling over the dough rectangle. Roll up the dough lengthwise. Cut the roll into twelve 1-inch-thick slices with the Serrated Bread Knife.

3. Place the slices in the Deep Dish Baker. Sprinkle with remaining filling.

4 cups canned pineapple chunks, drained

1 cup blueberries

1 medium cantaloupe

1 pint strawberries

1 lime

1 carton (8 ounces) plain yogurt

2 tablespoons honey

½ teaspoon vanilla extract

Tangy Fruit Salad with Sweet Yogurt Dressing

Combine pineapple and blueberries in Classic 2-Qt. Batter Bowl. Cut cantaloupe in half and remove seeds. Using Small Stainless Steel Scoop, form melon balls. Add to Batter Bowl. Remove hulls from strawberries with Tomato Corer. Using Egg Slicer, cut half the strawberries into thin slices and add to other fruit. Toss to combine. Using Food Chopper, finely chop remaining strawberries and place in 1-Quart Batter Bowl.

Remove zest from lime, using Lemon Zester/Scorer, and add to chopped strawberries. Use Lemon Aid to remove juice from lime. Add juice to chopped strawberries along with yogurt, honey and vanilla extract. Stir gently to combine.

Spoon fruit into 6 bowls. Serve dressing alongside fruit.

Yield: 6 servings

¼ cup chocolate sprinkles

8 large marshmallows

⅓ cup semisweet chocolate morsels

4 cups milk

¼ cup instant chocolate milk powder

Extra Special Hot Chocolate

Place chocolate sprinkles in Classic 2-Qt. Batter Bowl. One at time, run marshmallows under cold water, shake off excess water and use a spoon to roll in chocolate sprinkles. Place coated marshmallows on Kitchen Parchment and set aside.

In same Batter Bowl, combine semisweet chocolate and milk. Microwave on High 4 minutes. Add chocolate milk powder and mix with 10-inch Whisk until smooth. Microwave 3 more minutes or until hot. Whisk again, pour into 4 large mugs and top with marshmallows. Serve hot.

Yield: 4 servings

A Hearty Start

APPLE POPOVER PANCAKE • APPLE HARVEST SYRUP • SAUSAGE LINKS
POLYNESIAN COOLERS

Next time you're making hotcakes, why not do **one** for the entire family? This pie-sized pancake filled with a cinnamon-apple mixture is satisfying enough to feed the whole gang, especially if it's topped with the warm, apple-and-cinnamon-laced syrup.

Grocery List

3 large eggs
Milk
Butter
6 medium Granny Smith
  apples
Apple jelly

1 can (6 oz.) frozen
  orange juice concen-
  trate
Pineapple juice
Apricot nectar
Club soda

Pantry Items

Vegetable oil
All-purpose flour
Lemon
Sugar

Ground cinnamon
Maple syrup
Powdered sugar

Popover:

1 tablespoon vegetable oil

3 large eggs

½ cup milk

1 tablespoon butter or
    margarine, melted

½ cup all-purpose flour

Powdered sugar (optional)

Filling:

6 medium Granny Smith apples

1 tablespoon butter or margarine

1 tablespoon lemon juice

¼ cup sugar

½ teaspoon ground cinnamon

Apple Popover Pancake

Preheat oven to 450°F. Pour oil into Stoneware 9-inch Pie Plate. Using Pastry Brush, coat surface with oil. Combine eggs, milk and melted butter in 1-Quart Batter Bowl. Mix with 10-inch Whisk. Add flour and whisk until smooth. Pour batter into Pie Plate. Bake 13 minutes without opening oven door (pancake should be puffed up high around edges). Reduce oven temperature to 350°F and bake 15 more minutes or until sides are crisp.

Meanwhile, peel, core and slice apples. Cut slices in half. Melt butter in Stir-Fry Skillet over medium-high heat. Add apples, lemon juice, sugar and cinnamon. Cook, stirring gently, until apples are tender, about 4 minutes. Gently spoon apple mixture into pancake. Cut in wedges and serve immediately with Apple Harvest Syrup or dust lightly with powdered sugar.

Yield: 6 servings

1 cup maple syrup

½ cup apple jelly

¼ teaspoon ground cinnamon

Apple Harvest Syrup

Combine maple syrup, jelly and cinnamon in 1½-quart Generation II Saucepan. Bring to a simmer over low heat and cook 2 minutes. Serve warm.

Yield: 1½ cups

1 can (6 ounces) frozen orange juice
  concentrate

1½ cups pineapple juice, chilled

1½ cups apricot nectar, chilled

2½ cups club soda, chilled

Polynesian Coolers

Place orange juice concentrate, pineapple juice and apricot nectar in
Quick-Stir Pitcher. Plunge handle up and down until concentrate is
dissolved. Slowly pour in club soda. Gently plunge handle up and
down just until combined. Serve immediately.

Yield: 6 servings

Do-Ahead Tip:
If desired, combine all juices the night before in
Quick-Stir Pitcher and refrigerate. Just before serving,
add club soda and mix gently.

Pizza for Lunch

DELUXE TURKEY CLUB PIZZA • CARROT, CUCUMBER AND PEPPER STICKS
FRUIT SLUSH • SOFT DRINKS

Surprise your Saturday afternoon company with turkey, bacon and cheese served on an easy sesame-seed pizza crust—a great way to combine two all-time favorites in one lunch! Raw veggies presented in decorative pepper cups complete the meal.

Grocery List

1 can (10 oz.) Pillsbury
  Refrigerated All Ready
  Pizza Crust
Sesame seeds
1 cup shredded Monterey
  Jack cheese
Fresh basil
4 oz. deli turkey breast
  slices

Bacon
2 small plum tomatoes
½ cup shredded Swiss
  cheese
1 package fruit-flavored
  gelatin
3 cups pineapple juice

Pantry Items

Mayonnaise
Lemon   Sugar

Crust:

1 can (10 ounces) Pillsbury Refrigerated All Ready Pizza Crust

2 teaspoons sesame seeds

Topping:

¼ cup mayonnaise

1 teaspoon lemon zest

1 cup shredded Monterey Jack cheese

1 tablespoon thinly sliced fresh basil or 1 teaspoon dried basil

4 ounces deli turkey breast slices, cut into 1-inch strips

6 strips bacon, cut into 1-inch pieces, cooked

2 small plum tomatoes or 1 small tomato, thinly sliced

½ cup shredded Swiss cheese

Fresh basil leaves

Deluxe Turkey Club Pizza

Preheat oven to 425°F. Unroll dough and place on 13-inch Round Baking Stone. Starting at center, roll dough into a 12-inch circle, using Dough and Pizza Roller. Sprinkle sesame seeds evenly over dough. Bake 10 to 12 minutes or until crust is light golden brown.

Combine mayonnaise and lemon zest in a small bowl; blend well. Spread mixture over crust. Top with Monterey Jack cheese, sliced basil, turkey, bacon and tomatoes. Sprinkle with Swiss cheese. Bake 7 to 9 minutes or until crust is golden brown and cheese is melted. Garnish with basil leaves.

Yield: 6 to 8 servings

*If you like to cook, you'll **love** cooking with our stoneware. The even heat from the baking stone's surface makes it perfect for baking cookies and other treats, and the same is true of casseroles and cobblers made in the Stoneware Baking Bowl. And our stoneware just gets better with age: The more you use it, the more seasoned it becomes.*

½ cup sugar

¼ cup (½ package)
fruit-flavored gelatin

¾ cup boiling water

3 cups pineapple juice

Fruit Slush

Combine sugar, gelatin and water in Classic 2-Qt. Batter Bowl. Stir until gelatin is dissolved. Add pineapple juice. Divide mixture evenly among 3 Ice Shaver tubs. Freeze until firm. Remove from tubs and shave in Ice Shaver. Pile shaved ice into stemmed glasses or dessert bowls. Serve with a spoon.

Yield: 6 servings

Soup and Sandwich Combo

HOT SMOKED TURKEY SANDWICH • TOMATO SOUP
CHEESE CURLS • ORANGE DREAM DELIGHTS

For an easy but satisfying hot lunch after Saturday morning errands, serve Tomato Soup and these smoked turkey and Swiss cheese sandwiches with a do-ahead herbed mayonnaise, and heated on a Baking Stone just long enough for the cheese to melt.

Grocery List

Parsley
2 medium tomatoes
4 slices rye bread
½ lb. smoked turkey
¼ lb. Swiss cheese

1 can (6 oz.) frozen
orange juice
concentrate
Milk
Vanilla ice cream

Pantry Items

Mayonnaise
Dijon mustard

Dried oregano
Ground black pepper

Hot Smoked Turkey Sandwich

¼ cup mayonnaise

2 teaspoons Dijon mustard

2 tablespoons chopped parsley

½ teaspoon dried oregano

⅛ teaspoon ground black pepper

2 medium tomatoes

4 slices rye bread

½ pound smoked turkey, sliced

¼ pound Swiss cheese, sliced

Preheat oven to 350°F. In 1-Quart Batter Bowl, combine mayonnaise, mustard, parsley, oregano and pepper; mix well. Using Serrated Bread Knife, thinly slice tomatoes.

Place bread on 13-inch Round Baking Stone. Spread each slice with some of the mayonnaise mixture. Dividing evenly, place turkey slices on bread. Top with tomatoes and cheese. Bake 10 to 13 minutes or until cheese is browned and bubbling. Serve hot.

Yield: 4 servings

When you want to please finicky children, you can turn pouts into smiles with the help of some creative recipes, our kitchen tools and a few personal touches. It's easy to inject some whimsy into everyday dishes with fun shapes, cut-outs and combinations; your children will be so surprised and delighted, they won't even notice these foods are good for them too!

1 can (6 ounces) frozen orange juice
  concentrate

2¼ cups milk

2 large scoops vanilla ice cream

Orange Dream Delights

Place all ingredients in Quick-Stir Pitcher. Move plunger up and down until concentrate is dissolved and drink is thick and frothy. Pour into 4 tall glasses and serve.

Yield: 4 servings

Surprise Burgers

MONTEREY BURGERS • CARROT AND CELERY STICKS • OLD-FASHIONED POTATO SALAD
POPSICLES OR FRUIT POPS • SOFT DRINKS

Your children will burst into a grin when they bite into these tangy burgers and discover the cheesy surprise inside! Old-Fashioned Potato Salad, a perennial favorite, is given extra zing with the addition of cider vinegar, radishes and a smooth mustard-mayonnaise dressing.

Grocery List

2 medium onions
1 lb. ground round
Barbecue sauce
¼ lbs. shredded Monterey
Jack cheese

4 hamburger buns
1½ lbs. red potatoes
Celery
1 package radishes
1 small cucumber

Pantry Items

Salt
Ground black pepper
Mayonnaise

Mustard
Cider vinegar

Monterey Burgers

1 medium onion

1 pound ground round

2 tablespoons barbecue sauce

½ teaspoon salt

¼ teaspoon ground black pepper

¼ pound shredded Monterey Jack cheese

4 hamburger buns

Finely chop onion with Food Chopper. Combine onion, ground round, barbecue sauce, salt and pepper in Classic 2-Qt. Batter Bowl; mix well. Divide mixture into 4 equal portions. Shape each portion into a patty and press a fourth of the cheese into center of each. Pull sides of patty up and over cheese, enclosing cheese completely. Gently re-form each portion into a flat patty, making sure cheese does not poke out.

In 10-inch Generation II Frying Pan, cook patties over medium-high heat, turning once, until done: 3 minutes per side for medium-rare, 4 minutes per side for medium and 5 minutes per side for well done. Serve on hamburger buns.

Yield: 4 servings

Old-Fashioned Potato Salad

1½ pounds red potatoes

½ cup mayonnaise

1 tablespoon prepared mustard

2 teaspoons cider vinegar

1 celery stalk, diced

6 radishes, sliced

½ small cucumber, peeled

2 tablespoons finely chopped onion

Salt and ground black pepper to taste

Fill 4-quart Generation II Casserole with water and bring to a boil. Using 5-inch Self-Sharpening Utility Knife, cut potatoes into ½-inch cubes. Add to boiling water and cook until tender, about 10 minutes. Meanwhile, combine mayonnaise, mustard and vinegar in Classic 2-Qt. Batter Bowl with 10-inch Whisk. Add celery and radishes. Remove cucumber seeds by pushing Apple Corer through center of cucumber. Dice cucumber and add to Batter Bowl. Add onion and stir.

Drain and rinse potatoes under cold water. Add to cucumber mixture and fold in gently with Mix 'N Scraper. Season with salt and pepper and serve.

Yield: 4 to 6 servings

PB'n'A Pockets

PEANUT BUTTER AND APPLE POCKETS • PRETZELS
FRESH GRAPES • BLACK COWS

A *lunchtime staple becomes healthier when you substitute chopped apple or other fruit for the jelly. Let the kids seal the filling inside whole-wheat bread with the Cut-N-Seal, and you've got a portable, nutritious treat.*

Grocery List

1 small Granny Smith apple
1 small package (3 oz.) cream cheese
1 loaf soft white or wheat bread

Vanilla ice cream
Root beer
Whipped cream

Pantry Items

Peanut butter
Brown sugar

Ground cinnamon

1 small Granny Smith apple

¼ cup creamy peanut butter

1 small package (3 ounces) cream
cheese, at room temperature

2 tablespoons firmly packed brown
sugar

⅛ teaspoon ground cinnamon

1 loaf soft white or wheat bread

Peanut Butter and Apple Pockets

Using Apple Peeler/Corer/Slicer, peel, core and slice apple.
Chop prepared apple with Food Chopper. Combine apple,
peanut butter, cream cheese, brown sugar and cinnamon in
1-Quart Batter Bowl. Place a scant tablespoon of the filling in
center of a bread slice. Top with another bread slice. Repeat
until all filling is used. Use the 3-inch Cut-N-Seal to cut and
seal round sandwiches.

Yield: 12 sandwiches

Variation: Omit apple, brown sugar and cinnamon. Instead,
cut a banana with Egg Slicer; turn halfway and slice again to
make quarters. Combine banana, cream cheese, peanut butter
and 3 tablespoons strawberry jam in Batter Bowl and use
as directed above.

4 large scoops vanilla ice cream

4 cups cold root beer

Whipped cream (optional)

Black Cows

Place 1 scoop of the ice cream into each of 4 tall glasses. Pour root
beer over ice cream. Top with whipped cream, if desired. Add straws
and tall spoons. Serve immediately.

Yield: 4 servings

Old-Fashioned Favorites

MOM'S CHICKEN NOODLE SOUP • ASSORTED CRACKERS AND CHEESE
QUICK APPLE CRISP • MILK

Homemade chicken noodle soup doesn't have to cook forever to be delicious. As leftover chicken, chopped vegetables and pasta shells simmer, put together a cinnamon-y apple crisp—the perfect finish to a cozy, comforting lunch.

Grocery List
2 medium onions
2 carrots
Celery
Small pasta shells

2 cups cooked chicken
5 Granny Smith apples
1 small package (9oz.) yellow cake mix
Butter

Pantry Items
Chicken broth
Salt
Dill weed

Sugar
Ground cinnamon

80

Mom's Chicken Noodle Soup

3 cans (14½ ounces each)
  chicken broth

2 medium onions

2 carrots

1½ teaspoons salt

2 celery stalks, sliced

¾ cup small pasta shells

2 cups cooked, diced chicken

Snipped dill for garnish (optional)

In 4-quart Generation II Casserole, heat chicken broth to a simmer, covered. Meanwhile, coarsely chop onions with Food Chopper. Thinly slice carrots with Grater-Slicer.

Add salt, onions, carrots and celery to broth. Cover and simmer until vegetables are almost tender, about 5 minutes. Add pasta shells and cook, uncovered, stirring occasionally, for 8 minutes. Add chicken and cook until pasta is tender, about 3 more minutes. Ladle soup into 4 bowls. Garnish with dill, if desired. Serve hot.

Yield: 4 servings

Quick Apple Crisp

5 Granny Smith apples

1 small package (9 ounces)
  yellow cake mix

2 tablespoons sugar

1 tablespoon ground cinnamon

¼ cup butter or margarine,
  melted

Preheat oven to 350°F. Using Apple Peeler/Corer/Slicer, peel, core and slice apples. Place in Deep Dish Baker. Sprinkle dry cake mix over apples. Combine sugar and cinnamon in Flour/Sugar Shaker; sprinkle over cake mix. Drizzle with butter. Bake 30 to 35 minutes. Serve warm.

Yield: 8 to 12 servings

Variations: Add ¼ to ½ cup raisins, nuts or oats as desired.

I try to buy foods in their "least prepared" form—a whole chicken, rather than pieces of chicken, or whole mushrooms or olives, rather than the chopped version. The less prepared food is, the more economical—and you can use it for a wider variety of cooking needs.

Quick Quesadillas

CHICKEN QUESADILLAS • HEARTY BEAN SOUP
COOKIES • MILK

Fold leftover chicken, soup, cheese and, if you dare, a jalapeño pepper into flour tortillas. While they bake, stir some chopped vegetables and tomatoes into canned bean soup, and you've got a fun, south of the border lunch.

Grocery List

3 boneless, skinless chicken breast halves (about 12 oz.)
3 jalapeño peppers
1 can (10¾ oz.) Campbell's® Condensed Cream of Chicken Soup
1 cup shredded Cheddar cheese
Eight 8-inch flour tortillas

3 or 4 plum tomatoes
Fresh cilantro
Sour cream
1 medium onion
1 medium carrot
1 medium zucchini
1 can (11½ oz.) condensed bean with bacon soup
1 can (14½ oz.) diced tomatoes with garlic and onion

Pantry Items

Salsa
Olive oil

Salt
Ground black pepper

3 boneless, skinless chicken breast halves (about 12 ounces total), cooked

1 jalapeño pepper, seeded (optional)

1 can (10¾ ounces) Campbell's® Condensed Cream of Chicken Soup

1 cup shredded Cheddar cheese

8 flour tortillas (8 inches in diameter)

Fresh plum tomato slices

Jalapeño pepper slices

Cilantro sprigs

Salsa

Sour cream

Chicken Quesadillas

Preheat oven to 400°F. Chop chicken and, if using, jalapeño pepper with Food Chopper. Combine chicken, pepper, soup and ½ cup of the cheese in Classic 2-Qt. Batter Bowl. Mix well. Using Super Scraper, spread ¼ cup of the soup mixture over half of each tortilla to within ½ inch of edge. With Pastry Brush, moisten edge of each tortilla with water, fold over and press edges together.

Place tortillas on 15-inch Round Baking Stone. Bake 8 minutes or until hot. Sprinkle with remaining cheese. Using Pizza Cutter, cut into wedges. Arrange on a serving plate and garnish with tomato slices, pepper slices and cilantro. Serve with salsa and sour cream.

Yield: 8 quesadillas or 32 appetizer servings

---

1 teaspoon olive oil

1 medium onion, chopped

1 medium carrot, chopped

1 medium zucchini, chopped

1 can (11½ ounces) condensed bean with bacon soup

1 can water

1 can (14½ ounces) diced tomatoes with garlic and onion

Salt and ground black pepper to taste

Hearty Bean Soup

Heat oil in 2-quart Generation II Saucepan over medium-high heat. Add onion and carrot. Sauté until onion is transparent, about 5 minutes. Stir in zucchini and sauté 1 more minute. Stir in soup, water and tomatoes. Bring to a simmer and cook 3 minutes. Season with salt and pepper. Ladle into 4 bowls and serve.

Yield: 4 servings

Snacks

Peanut Butter Crispy Treats • Apple Berry Salsa with Cinnamon Crisps • Crunchy Fruit and Vegetable Pick-Ups • Toasted Coconut Snowballs • Peanut Buster Pizza Vanilla Popcorn • Spiced Party Popcorn

These are perfect homemade snacks to welcome the kids home from school even if you can't be there to greet them. Surprise them with one of these easy munchies: popcorn sweetened with cinnamon, sugar and fruit; "pizza" made from brownie mix; fruity salsa served with cinnamon "chips"; or fruits and veggies that look fancy but taste naturally delicious.

Peanut Butter Crispy Treats

¼ cup butter or margarine

1 package (10 ounces) marshmallows (about 40 large)

¼ cup creamy peanut butter

½ cup chopped peanuts

5 cups oven-toasted rice cereal

Nonstick vegetable spray

Melt butter in Stir-Fry Skillet over medium heat. Add marshmallows and stir with Bamboo Spoon until softened. Add peanut butter and peanuts; stir until smooth. Remove from heat and gradually stir in cereal until well coated.

Spray 2 Valtrompia Bread Tubes with nonstick vegetable spray and pack mixture into tubes. Let cool about 30 minutes before removing. Slice to serve.

Yield: About 24 slices

Variations:

Omit peanut butter, if desired.

Substitute ¼ cup cinnamon candies or ½ cup chopped English toffee candy bar for peanuts and stir into marshmallow mixture before adding cereal.

Apple Berry Salsa with Cinnamon Crisps

2 flour tortillas (10 inches in diameter)

1 tablespoon granulated sugar

1 teaspoon ground cinnamon

1 Granny Smith apple

1 cup strawberries

1 kiwi, peeled

1 small orange

2 tablespoons brown sugar

2 tablespoons apple jelly

Preheat oven to 475°F. Brush tortillas with water, using Pastry Brush. Combine granulated sugar and cinnamon in Flour/Sugar Shaker; sprinkle over tortillas. Using Kitchen Cutters, cut each tortilla into 8 wedges and place on 15-inch Round Baking Stone. Bake 5 to 7 minutes or until golden brown. Let cool on Non-Stick Cooling Rack.

Using Apple Peeler/Corer/Slicer, peel, core and slice apple. Cut into quarters and chop with Food Chopper. Hull strawberries and kiwi with Tomato Corer. Slice strawberries with Egg Slicer. Chop kiwi with Food Chopper. Remove zest from orange, using Lemon Zester/Scorer. Use Lemon Aid to remove juice from orange. Combine prepared fruit, orange zest, orange juice, brown sugar and apple jelly in a bowl. Serve fruit salsa with cinnamon crisps.

Yield: 8 servings

Grocery List

2 celery stalks
2 medium apples
1 cucumber
Cream cheese
Spreadable cheese
Chopped dried fruit
Chopped nuts
Sunflower seeds
Granola

Pantry Items

Peanut butter

2 stalks celery

2 medium apples

1 cucumber

Spreads:

Cream cheese, at room
temperature

Peanut butter

Spreadable cheese, at room
temperature

Toppings:

Chopped dried fruit

Chopped nuts

Sunflower seeds

Granola

Crunchy Fruit and Vegetable Pick-Ups

Using 3-inch Self-Sharpening Paring Knife, cut celery into 3-inch sticks. If desired, fan an end of each celery stick, using Egg Slicer: Push end of celery halfway through Egg Slicer's wires and remove; give celery a quarter turn and push halfway through wires again. Place celery in Classic 2-Qt. Batter Bowl filled with ice water to fan. Blot celery dry before filling with spread.

Using Apple Wedger, cut apples into wedges.

Using Lemon Zester/Scorer, score down length of cucumber at ¼-inch intervals to remove several narrow strips of peel.* Cut into ½-inch slices with Garnisher.

Pipe desired spread onto fruit and vegetable pieces, using Easy Accent Decorator. Sprinkle with desired topping. Serve immediately.

Yield: 4 servings

* For extra flair, after scoring cucumber, remove seeds by
  pushing Apple Corer through center of cucumber. Dry
  inside of cucumber with a paper towel. Pipe desired spread
  directly into center of cucumber. Slice as directed above.

Making the Cheese and Cucumber Rings

1. Dry the centers of cucumbers that have been scored with the Lemon Zester/Scorer and cored with the Apple Corer.

2. Fill the centers of cucumbers with cheese using the Easy Accent Decorator. Slice the cucumbers into rings with the Garnisher.

1 cup coconut

15 large marshmallows

Toasted Coconut Snowballs

Preheat oven to 350°F. Spread coconut
on 13-inch Round Baking Stone and
bake 7 to 9 minutes, stirring occasionally, until evenly browned.
Transfer to 1-Quart Batter Bowl and let cool.

One at a time, run marshmallows under cold water,
shake off excess water and drop into coconut. Using your fingers,
press coconut onto marshmallows. Place on Kitchen Parchment and
let dry 30 minutes before serving.

Yield: 15 snowballs

1 package (19.8 ounces) brownie mix

1 package (8 ounces) cream cheese,
    at room temperature

½ cup firmly packed brown sugar

¼ cup creamy peanut butter

2 packages (1.6 ounces each)
    peanut butter cups

¼ cup peanuts

2 bananas

1 ounce chocolate

2 teaspoons butter or margarine

Peanut Buster Pizza

Preheat oven to 350°F. In Classic
2-Qt. Batter Bowl, prepare brownie
mix according to package directions.
Place a piece of Kitchen Parchment
on 15-inch Round Baking Stone.
Pour brownie mixture on paper and
spread into a 14-inch circle. (Do not
bake without Parchment Paper or
batter will run off stone during baking.)
Bake 20 to 25 minutes or until set. Let cool completely.

Mix cream cheese, brown sugar and peanut butter until smooth.
Spread over brownie "crust." Chop peanut butter cups and
peanuts with Food Chopper and sprinkle over peanut butter
mixture. Using Egg Slicer, slice bananas and layer over peanuts.
Place chocolate and butter in Micro-Cooker and microwave
on High for 1 minute and 30 seconds; stir until smooth. Using
V-Shaped Cutter, drizzle mixture over pizza. Cut into squares
with Pizza Cutter and serve.

Yield: 16 servings

8 cups plain popped popcorn*

4 teaspoons powdered sugar

¼ teaspoon salt

4 drops vanilla extract

Vanilla Popcorn

Pour popcorn into Stoneware Baking Bowl. Put sugar and salt into Flour/Sugar Shaker. Shake over popcorn and toss well. Sprinkle with vanilla, toss again and serve.

Yield: 4 servings

* You may substitute 1 bag (2.85 ounces) natural microwave popcorn, popped. Omit salt if using microwave popcorn.

Grocery List
8 cups popcorn

Pantry Items
Powdered sugar
Salt
Vanilla extract

8 cups plain popped popcorn*

½ cup diced mixed dried fruit

4 teaspoons powdered sugar

½ teaspoon ground cinnamon

¼ teaspoon salt

Spiced Party Popcorn

Pour popcorn into Stoneware Baking Bowl. Add dried fruit and stir. Put sugar, cinnamon and salt into Flour/Sugar Shaker. Shake over popcorn mixture, toss well and serve.

Yield: 4 servings

* You may substitute 1 bag (2.85 ounces) natural microwave popcorn, popped. Omit salt if using microwave popcorn.

Grocery List
8 cups popcorn
½ cup mixed dried fruit

Pantry Items
Powdered sugar
Ground cinnamon
Salt

Making the Radish Mouse *(as shown on page 84)*

1. Cut two slices from one of the round radishes, to make the ears.

2. Push a toothpick halfway into the "body" of the radish mouse (shown above). Then cut two V-shaped grooves in the "head" of the mouse and place the mouse ears in these notches. Carefully place the mouse "head" on the toothpick.

3. For the whiskers, cut ¾-inch pieces from the ends of toothpicks and poke the blunt ends into the "head." Use cloves for the eyes.

Timesaving Kitchen Tools from The Pampered Chef

Cutting Boards
Safe, sanitary polyethylene cutting boards that won't dull knives or harbor odors or bacteria.

Self-Sharpening Knives
Self-sharpens each time you pull knife out of holder. High quality triple riveted handle.

Vegetable Peeler
Stainless steel, swivel action blade; use left- or right-handed.

Garnisher
Completely constructed of stainless steel with easy-grip plastic handle. Crinkle cut fruits, vegetables and cheeses.

Kitchen Cutters
Strong shears that stay sharp; holder keeps them handy. Great for "mincing" fresh herbs.

Cheese Slicer
High quality German slicer cuts two different widths of cheese. Attractive styling.

Lemon Zester/Scorer
Combination tool cuts fine shreds of peel from citrus fruit for baking and cuts long strips for twists.

V-Shaped Cutter
Separates fruits or vegetables into two fluted halves.

Tomato Corer
Commercial stainless steel tool quickly and neatly removes stem end of any size tomato.

Cut-N-Seals
Stainless steel, round tools cut and seal bread or pastry to make tarts or turnovers.

Pizza Cutter with Sleeve
Professional quality; 4-inch stainless steel blade; plastic handle. Includes protective storage sleeve for blade.

Oven Mitt and Baker's Pad
Oven Mitt features 100% thick cotton terry exterior with cotton padding insulation. Baker's Pad is 9- x 11-inch double-thick terry cloth.

Flat Baking Stones
Unglazed ceramic stones are used like baking sheets; absorb moisture and provide even heat. Great for pizzas, breads and cookies; reheating and crisping.

Oven-To-Table Racks
Nickel-plated steel; fits 13- or 15-inch Round Baking Stone and 12- x 15-inch Rectangle Stone.

Deep Dish Baker and Stoneware Baking Bowl
The unglazed, ceramic Deep Dish Baker is great for pies and quiches. Use the Stoneware Baking Bowl for casseroles and cobblers, or as a lid to create a covered clay baker.

Dough and Pizza Roller
Roll out dough with one hand. Unique design allows you to roll dough right in the pan. Great for pizza, pastry or cookie dough. Easy for kids to handle.

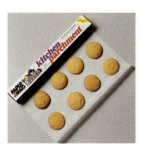

Kitchen Parchment
Roll of nonstick paper to line baking pans.

Non-Stick Cooling Rack
Generous 10- x 18-inch black grid rack for cooling baked goods.

Pastry Brush
Boar bristles can withstand exposure to hot foods. Hook allows brush to hang on edge of bowl for added convenience.

All-Purpose Icing Spreader
Great tool for icing cakes or spreading sandwiches. Stainless steel blade, plastic handle.

Skinny, Super and Mix 'N Scrapers
Even hot spaghetti sauce won't stain these durable silicone scrapers.

Bamboo Spoon Set
10-inch, 12-inch and 14-inch spoons are sturdy and dishwasher safe.

Pastry Blender
The perfect tool for evenly cutting fat into flour for light and flaky pie crusts. Stainless steel construction.

Flour/Sugar Shaker
Stainless steel screen; 1 cup size; dusts flour, powdered sugar, cinnamon sugar. Includes storage cap.

Easy Accent Decorator

Our exclusive design makes it easy to get professional results even if you are a beginner. Includes six different tips for use with frosting, fillings, soft cheese spreads or even peanut butter.

Stir-Fry Skillet

A unique, flat-bottomed wok/skillet combination with a generous 12-inch diameter. Heavy-gauge aluminum with DuPont SilverStone Select nonstick coating inside and durable enamel finish outside.

Tool Turn-About

Organize your kitchen utensils and have them within easy reach with this rotating storage container.

Adjustable Scoop

The perfect companion to the Adjustable Measuring Spoons. This measuring scoop adjusts from ⅛ cup to ½ cup.

Salt and Pepper Mill

Stylish pepper mill with adjustable grind operates one-handed for the busy cook.

Adjustable Measuring Spoons

Set of two. Small spoon adjusts from ⅛ to 1 teaspoon. Large spoon adjusts from 1 teaspoon to 1 tablespoon.

Classic 2-Qt. and 1-Quart Batter Bowls

Measure, mix and pour in the same bowl. Both measuring bowls feature oven proof glass, spout, handle and a micro-wavable plastic lid.

3-Way Tongs

Unbreakable tongs can be used three different ways. Great for tossing and serving salads and pasta. Dishwasher safe. Lifetime guarantee against breakage.

Pocket Thermometer

Instant-read thermometer measures from 0°-220°F. Essential for proper yeast temperatures and for cooking meats.

Quick-Stir Pitcher

The ingenious plunger in this 2-quart pitcher mixes cans of frozen concentrate juice and water—and you don't have to thaw the juice first! Also great for kid's powdered drink mixes.

Lemon Aid

Keeps fresh lemon juice handy at all times. Now with larger storage container.

11-inch Square Griddle

From the Generation II collection with DuPont SilverStone Select nonstick finish. Great for panckaes!

12-inch Family Skillet

From the Generation II collection with DuPont SilverStone Select nonstick finish. The ideal pan for family-sized meals.

Apple Corer

Chrome blade does a thorough job of coring apples for snacking or baking.

Apple Wedger

Stainless steel blades; cores and slices an apple or pear into eight sections.

Apple Peeler/Corer/ Slicer and Stand

Peels, cores and slices a firm apple in 30 seconds. Makes perfect slices for desserts, salads and snacks; the Stand makes it easier to use.

10-inch Whisk

Professional quality, stainless steel whisk comes with manufacturer's lifetime guarantee.

Stainless Steel Scoops

Heavy duty scoops are ideal for melon balls, cookies and more. 1¼- or 1¾-inch diameter.

Garlic Press

Swiss peeler crushes fresh garlic cloves with ease. Best of all, you don't have to peel the clove before crushing!

Food Chopper

Fast, easy, efficient chopping of vegetables, nuts, fruits; opens for easy cleaning.

Mini-Serving Spatula

Stainless steel blade, plastic handle; ideal for serving desserts and appetizers.

Covered Micro-Cooker

Handy 1-quart pan includes a vented lid and pouring spouts for added convenience. 4-cup volume.

Chillzanne Platter

Iceless, cold platter with frosted dome lid keeps food cold for hours. Generous 15-inch diameter. Great for transporting food to picnics or parties.

Ice Cream Dipper and Ice Shaver

Defrosting liquid sealed in handle makes scooping ice cream easy! Ice Shaver creates homemade snow cones and slushes.

Index